Wayward Women

For Lorin

Wayward Women

Female Offending in Victorian England

Lucy Williams

PEN & SWORD
HISTORY

First published in Great Britain in 2016 by
Pen & Sword History
an imprint of
Pen & Sword Books Ltd
47 Church Street
Barnsley
South Yorkshire
S70 2AS

ISBN 978 1 47384 487 2

A CIP catalogue record for this book is available from the British
Library.

Typeset in Ehrhardt by
Mac Style Ltd, Bridlington, East Yorkshire
Printed and bound in the UK by CPI Group (UK) Ltd,
Croydon, CRO 4YY

Pen & Sword Books Ltd incorporates the imprints of Pen & Sword
Archaeology, Atlas, Aviation, Battleground, Discovery, Family
History, History, Maritime, Military, Naval, Politics, Railways, Select,
Transport, True Crime, and Fiction, Frontline Books, Leo Cooper,
Praetorian Press, Seaforth Publishing and Wharncliffe.

For a complete list of Pen & Sword titles please contact
PEN & SWORD BOOKS LIMITED
47 Church Street, Barnsley, South Yorkshire, S70 2AS, England
E-mail: enquiries@pen-and-sword.co.uk
Website: www.pen-and-sword.co.uk

Contents

Acknowledgements

The opportunity to write this book came somewhat out of the blue but has been an enjoyable and rewarding challenge all the more for it. I want to express my gratitude to a number of people for all the help and encouragement they offered along the way.

The first of my thanks has to go to the team at Pen and Sword who saw the potential in this project, gave a chance to a first-time author, and guided me through the whole process.

As a seasoned author herself, and brilliant academic of gender and crime, Nell Darby offered much encouragement and advice on how to source some good pictures, for which I am very grateful. I have been lucky to be able to include some fantastic photos, along with the stories of female offending, with permission from the Tasmanian Archive and Heritage Office, Harvard Broadside Collections, and The National Archives. My thanks go to them.

There is also a long list of people who have encouraged me and propped me up for years while I played with the stories of *Wayward Women* – from its earliest days as a blog, to the printed book. Mike McGibney lent invaluable support and constructive criticism in the early phases of writing, for which I owe thanks to both him and his trusty red pen. He is also a wonderful and generous friend, never ceasing to make time for my endeavors even when his plate is overflowing with his own. Kate Hales, Sara Fisher and Lesley Williams have shared in my hopes and fears as I put this book together, which has made it an altogether more exciting prospect. They have also all assured me that they will be first in line to buy a copy – which never hurts.

My final and biggest thanks go to Lorin Davies, who pushed me to 'go for it' as soon as the chance came along, who kept me fed and watered as I wrote, and who celebrated every little triumph along the way with me. He also lent a valuable pair of eyes over the first draft. He encourages me to pursue every opportunity and to be my very best self. This book is for him.

Introduction

Infamous Creatures

I cannot remember the first time I set eyes on a picture of a Victorian female offender or listened, wide-eyed, to a tale of her escapades. All I know is that from the first time I heard of the Victorian murderess or the urchin-girl pickpocket she seemed exotic. The deeds of the female offender were no more remarkable or thought provoking than those of the plain old Victorian murderer or gentleman thief; it was rather that she herself seemed extraordinary. Our earliest learning about Victorian women is all corsets and crinolines, and ladies with lace parasols. Women who committed crime in this period seem so at odds with everything else we know about Victorian England. Perhaps that is why female offenders are so inherently fascinating – not just for me, but for many people who stumble across them.

Finding examples of deviant Victorian women is relatively easy. The very idea of them makes for a great story. You have almost certainly read about them. You will have seen them in films and on television too. Our modern appetite for dramas where the dresses are ragged and the deeds diabolical has a history stretching back more than 150 years. The Victorians themselves had a fair interest in wayward women too. They provided us with the narratives of death and deceit that still make best-selling books today; the slippery femme fatale who seduced her victims before she struck, the inhuman murderess from whom no soul was safe, and the sneak who killed from the shadows using poison as her weapon of choice. It was the Victorians also who first encouraged us to laugh at the ridiculous spectacle of the woman who committed crime, or to weep for her misfortune. That polite lady shoplifter, the kleptomaniac who stowed all manner of bizarre items beneath her petticoats, or the tragic wretches who were dragged in and undone by the world of male vice are characters so good they write themselves. One particular type of female offender has become, perhaps, literature and theatre's most recognisable stock character – the gutsy prostitute. Toughened by life's knocks, she nevertheless manages to maintain a gentle, sentimental side. The original tart with a heart was a Victorian. Whether we realise it or not we are so familiar with ideas about Victorian female offenders that we even know some of them by name, such as Nancy, Tess, or Fantine. (See plate 1.)

What we know of Victorian female offenders, we know well, with their tales so often having been told and retold to us in a thousand different guises. However, there is much more to their world than meets the eye. There are still many new stories emerging and more to know about Victorian women and their crimes. The full world of female offending in this period is one that we have seldom seen. Far from being just a set of stock characters, replaying the same stories over and again, the crimes that women perpetrated were diverse, revealing types of activity that still have the capacity to shock and surprise. Victorian female offenders can often remind us, more than we care to admit, of our own modern age.

I have been lucky enough to spend the last few years studying the lives and crimes of female offenders in England as an academic. There really is an enormous amount to say on the matter. However, this book is not that. It is not an exhaustive academic tome to explore and lay to rest the history of women and crime. Instead, *Wayward Women* is for anyone who, like me, is interested in crime in the Victorian period. It is for anyone who feels a tingle of curiosity on hearing one of the well-known stories of female offending in the foggy lamplit streets of Victorian England. For anyone who wonders if there is something more to tell. Within the pages of this book, you will find an introduction to some of the most fascinating, shocking and unexplored facets of female offending. Most importantly, you will find tales of women who could be brave and ruthless, frightening and fierce, sad, tragic and cunning. From violent acts and desperate thefts, to an overview of the different roles women played in the infamous Victorian sex trade, this book explores cases of the crimes we know well, and those that we have yet to discover.

Before we dive into the various crimes of Victorian wayward women, it might be helpful to know a little bit more about the world in which they lived, and what remains of them for us to find.

Above all else, two things dominated the experiences of women in Victorian England – social ideals about gender and class. The Victorian period was one of sharp contrasts: immense wealth and grinding poverty, as well as innovation and progress beside staunch traditionalism. Victorian society rested on traditional religious values, yet at the same time, it produced scientific enquiry the likes of which the world had never seen. Never was the contrast that existed between expectation, intention and reality more apparent than in the case of women.

The angel of the house and the devil in the street: Victorians and gender

The Victorian era was most certainly one in which men were expected to live up to traditional ideals of masculinity and women were expected to achieve the feminine ideal. It was a time before universal suffrage, before the 'sexual revolution' of the 1960s and before many of the equalities we take for granted today. So much of our own understanding of gender, of masculinity and femininity, can be traced back to the Victorians. Even in the twenty-first century, the experience of what it means to be a man or woman can be heavily shaped by our nineteenth-century roots – from equal pay and childcare, to the world of romance and dating.

In Victorian England, a divide between men and women was very clear. Perceptions of masculinity and femininity governed a good deal of everyday life. Gender norms ranged from the superficial, which saw dresses and corsets dominate women's fashion, to the deep-seated and ideological, which prescribed where women went, how they conducted themselves, and what they were able to do with their lives. According to these prevalent social ideals, women were, wherever possible, expected to conduct their lives in private. Women were supposed to lead a life based on home and family, where domestic duties took priority over anything else. When women did have to work, not all employments were open to them. Ideas about both their physical and mental frailty meant that paid work for women centred on the same sorts of tasks that they would carry out in the home: domestic service, laundry, dressmaking and cleaning.

Women were thought of as not only physically delicate and suited to a life at home, but also overly emotional and naive, and as such in need of the protection that home and husband could provide. A woman was assumed to possess innately all the qualities that made her an ideal helpmeet to a man. Where men were understood to be aggressive, virulent, strong and intelligent (although prone to moral weakness), women were passive, obedient, chaste, loving, faithful, moral, nurturing and maternal. From a Victorian perspective, above all, women were perceived to have been designed to be wives and mothers. In England during this time the perfect woman was the one that could live up to this domestic ideal. She was the 'angel in the house' of Coventry Patmore's famed poem, who loved and cared for her children, served her husband and lived a morally righteous, domesticated life. The ideal woman never spoke cross words, indulged in drink or questioned the authority of her husband or father. She was sexually passive, moral in all things and devoted to the needs of others. The woman who sat in a clean and ordered home, surrounded by rosy-cheeked children, sewing a bible psalm in cross stitch was well on her way to achieving the status of an ideal woman and could safely be placed on a pedestal by the rest of society.

Of course, the feminine ideal was not only highly unrealistic and difficult to achieve, but boring too. Raucous drinking, pre- or extra-marital sex and independence were all out of bounds to those who sought approval. Those women who never managed to cultivate the qualities of ideal womanhood, or did not care to try, could face stern disapproval and at times serious repercussions. Women who failed to live up to the ideal and flouted the very ideas upon which it was based had a name too. They were the opposite of the angel in the house; they were 'fallen' women. Anyone who failed to live up to social expectations could be denounced as fallen, but especially those who surrendered their virtue, their respectability or their morality. A woman considered fallen might be an unwed mother who had dared to engage in pre-marital sex, or a woman who provided back-street abortions. Stigma could be attached to any woman who refused or was unable to live up to the standard of acceptable femininity set for her. At best, these women would receive scorn for their transgressions and suffer a serious wound to their reputations; at worst, they could face social ostracism and even incarceration.

Female offenders were the very definition of fallen women. Whether they were prostitutes displaying their carnal lusts, thieves with no regard for morality, or violent viragoes who lived lives of physicality and aggression rather than passivity and softness, female offenders most certainly broke the rules when it came to expectations of women. Behaviours like drunkenness and lewdness were undesirable, but understandable in men. However, in a woman, drunkenness or obscene conduct might become more than just deviant – it could become criminal. A typical example of this behavioural double standard is prostitution. Both the prostitute and her customer were engaging in an act that posed an affront to Victorian moral and sexual sensibilities. Yet whilst her customer would face no reprisal, the prostitute could face arrest and imprisonment. It was not only in tipping the balance between deviance and crime that gender ideals might put women at a disadvantage, there is evidence to suggest that when a woman found herself on trial for transgressing the law, she might be judged more harshly than her male equivalent. Female offenders, it has been suggested, were not only guilty of breaking the criminal law, they were 'doubly deviant' as they had breached the unwritten moral code of social expectation too. This might lead to advanced likelihood of arrest and prosecution, less sympathy from a jury and a fuller penalty for some offences.

The fallen outcasts of low haunts: Victorians and class

No great secret has been made of the fact that the history of crime is usually, more accurately, the history of the working classes and crime. Just as gender differences were keenly felt in Victorian society, the class divide did not sit easily either. The nineteenth century was a period devoid of a welfare state, minimum wage or universal access to education. England was a country of the 'haves' and 'have nots'. Whilst the lucky few flourished and amassed huge private wealth, others lived in appalling poverty and degradation, and sometimes the two groups were neighbours living just a few miles away from each other within the same city. In general terms, this made for an atmosphere of fear and distrust between the different social classes. The working classes resented the power, wealth and control of social elites and the middle classes. Conversely, the elites and middle classes viewed the working class with distrust – after all, a small but vocal minority of them preached socialism, revolution and equality.

To a significant number of those in Parliament, the criminal justice system and the print media, the elevated level of crime amongst the working classes was not indicative of the harsh circumstances in which they lived and the fact that the vast majority of crime related to chronic want. Instead it was seen as evidence of innate criminality amongst the poor. As property owners themselves, judges and juries in court were unlikely to be sympathetic towards the labourer who burgled a middle-class house. Likewise, those who informed policing policy demanded that, as the element of society likely to be more criminal, those who lived in working-class areas and communities should receive more police attention. The result of this prejudice was the development of a criminal justice system based on suspicion of the poor, heightened attention on working-class areas and, as such, conformation of ideas about class and crime. Victorian England was, therefore, a place that saw working-class men and women more likely to offend because of chronic need and deprivation. It was also heavily policed, so working-class offenders were more likely to be caught if they committed a crime. Similarly, working-class men and women were much more likely than their middle-class peers to be convicted if they found themselves in court. As such, the working classes constituted the overwhelming majority of those in local and convict prisons, or those transported or sentenced to death. Unsurprisingly, statistics of the day supported the idea that crime was a working-class problem and validated decisions to target police attention on working-class communities and practices. It was a vicious and perpetual cycle.

I cannot dispute for one moment, nor do I wish to, that the vast majority of women who passed through Victorian England's courts and prisons were working-class women. For these women, crime plays an essential role in both their individual and collective history. However, rather than reproducing the long outdated and disproved Victorian ideas about how and why the working classes were those most often convicted of offending, the relationship between class and crime must be understood as part of a wider history of social conflict, power inequality and wealth disparity.

If only one knows where to look

So, where do we find real accounts of Victorian England's female offenders? To the joy of professional researchers and family historians alike, evidence of the distant past is no longer the preserve of dusty archives. A lot of information, particularly for the nineteenth century, is just a few clicks away for anyone with a computer. The majority of the cases in this book have come from digitised and fully name searchable sources. One of the best resources for learning about women and crime in the Victorian period remains the Old Bailey Online, which offers full transcripts of trials from London's Central Criminal Court. The Old Bailey covers offences as diverse as breaking the peace, fraud, arson, coining (making and distributing counterfeit money) and murder. A number of the cases in this book are drawn from court accounts, with context provided by supplementary social and criminal records. However, the story of women and crime in Victorian England is not just the story of London. Whilst contemporary accounts from the likes of social investigators such as Henry Mayhew and William Booth drew most of their inspiration from pacing the streets and back alleys of England's capital, there were many examples of every kind of crime occurring up and down the country. National newspaper reports, criminal registers and prison records give us valuable insight into the lives and crimes of female offenders throughout the country and provide other invaluable material for a history of this kind. Unfortunately, big cities, where the crime rates were highest, tend to have more historical records than smaller, more rural locations. The coverage of crime in England's many villages and townships is limited but wherever possible, stories of women in these places have also been included.

The very nature of the historian's craft is fragmentary and incomplete. Even the mass of evidence available for the most notorious cases in history cannot fill every gap. The fascinating cases of crime in this book, and the equally fascinating individuals responsible for them, are all real. The descriptions of the cases are from as many different accounts as possible in order to get the best sense of them. Criminal accounts are supplemented with evidence that relates details of offenders' personal lives. Records of birth, marriage and death, census records and, in rare cases, even personal correspondence are used. Where inferences are made about the women and their crimes, they are based upon the best possible evidence. Nothing about the cases in this book has been invented or supplemented with fiction.

Reader beware

Those interested in the history of crime and offenders have a better chance than ever before to uncover the who, what and how of offending in the nineteenth century. The names and stories of offenders sing out to us from criminal records, court testimony and newspaper coverage. However, we must always remember that the offenders we collect from our sources only ever show us a particular version of crime and its consequences.

The women we know about are largely those who were not the most gifted when it came to offending. The women who filled the courts and prisons in Victorian England – or any time and place for that matter – are those who have been identified and apprehended. By that very virtue we know that they were not the best criminals. The women whose stories are told in this book are those who made fundamental errors in perpetrating their crimes or concealing their deeds: coiners who attempted to pass bad currency in the same shop three days running; prostitutes whose public indiscretion or inability to move from a particular area saw them become easily recognised and repeatedly targeted by the police; and scorned women who attacked their victim in broad daylight in front of witnesses. We only know about their crimes and how they were carried out because the police did too.

The truly 'successful' offenders were those who left no trace of their activities or their names on formal records. Sometimes it is easy for us to see where the mistakes that led to capture and prosecution were made and we know that the offence would have been much the same for those who were never caught. Other times we must accept that there were ways and means of perpetrating crime that we know little if anything about. As well as giving us an insight into the world of female offending in the Victorian era, the cases in this book are without exception examples of how women came into contact with the police, courts and prisons. These female offenders are broadly representative of most women prosecuted for crime in Victorian England but we just don't know how well they represented all women who offended. Laurel Thatcher Ulrich is famed for writing the immortal lines 'well-behaved women seldom make history', but in the case of this history, we'd do well to remember that neither do those 'badly behaved' women who were truly capable of and talented in the ways of crime.

Into darkest England

The four chapters in this book will introduce a selection of crimes and the women who committed them. Somewhat oddly, our journey begins at where crime usually ends, with punishment, telling you all you need to know about potential consequences of crime in the Victorian period. After that, the chapters divide a range of offences into three main categories: crimes of property, violence and public order. The division of crime and offenders here is admittedly a little arbitrary. For the most part, crimes fit neatly into the categories of violence, theft and disorder – but who can really say where a violent robbery or theft by prostitutes really belongs? Likewise, offenders are rarely so obliging as to fit themselves into a neat category. A crime of theft might be only part of a life that involved drunkenness, disorder and violence.

Without further ado, let us descend into the world that famed Salvation Army devotee William Booth called 'Darkest England' and meet the women that could be found there.

Chapter 1

Locked Away, Sent Away, Launched into Eternity

Punishment in Victorian England

I t might have taken decades and countless history books but here in modern Britain we have finally come to the realisation that most things were not better in the past. Putting away the rose-tinted glasses when it comes to thinking about the Victorian stance on marriage and gender, on working hours and fair pay, on healthcare, voting rights and education is long overdue. It turns out that backbreaking manual labour and a world with no old-age pensions was not an easier lot than what we have now. We don't have to look particularly hard to find evidence that proves Victorian England could be a difficult and unfair place in which to live. However, whether it's politicians waxing lyrical about 'new policies' on the television, or simply snatched pieces of conversation in bus stop lines and supermarket queues, one area in which we refuse to relinquish the belief that our forebears had it right is when it comes to crime and punishment. The very phrase 'tough on crime, tough on criminals' brings back to us images of a bygone era when the law ruled with an iron fist and showed no mercy to society's bad apples – an image that is inescapably Victorian.

If there is one thing no one could accuse the Victorians of it is being soft on crime. The nineteenth century seems to have been a period in which statesmen, judges and philanthropists spent more time debating and devising what to do with criminals than any other time before or since. From the 1830s to the dawn of the twentieth century, three types of penalty dominated the justice system in England: imprisonment, transportation and capital punishment. Before we delve into the world of women and crime in Victorian England it is worth considering the fate that awaited many female offenders.

Locked away

One of the most renowned achievements of the Victorian age is the birth of the modern prison system. Those undergoing imprisonment in twenty-first century England share more in common with their Victorian predecessors than we might imagine. The ideals of punishment, reform and redemption first mooted by the Victorians are still prominent in discussions of prison and prisoners today. The practicalities of prison life are not wholly different either. Prisons today still function on a basic system of privileges and punishments, where inmates are given rights in return for taking on certain responsibilities. What's more, modern prisoners can even find themselves within the same buildings, treading the same halls, as the Victorian incarcerated. Institutions such as Brixton, Strangeways, Pentonville, Wormwood Scrubs and Holloway are still in use as prisons today and serve as an iconic reminder of Victorian penal innovation. (See plate 2.) The Victorians were responsible for inventing everything from the idea of prison uniforms to the parole system.

The rise of prisons to become the dominant form of punishment in Victorian England was a unique episode in history. The previous centuries had seen a criminal justice system that used a range of corporal and capital punishments. Gaols and 'lock-ups' did exist but acted as little more than holding pens for those awaiting trial, whipping, branding or hanging. Offenders could be held in houses of correction in various locations in England as punishment but these cases were relatively uncommon and did not stretch to long terms of incarceration. The most famous pre-Victorian prison was Newgate – a large gaol that held the accused awaiting trial in London, the convicted awaiting transportation and those awaiting the noose at Tyburn. Newgate, like other pre-Victorian prisons, was not intended to punish or reform, but primarily to detain – both men and women of all ages mixed together. Some were already convicted; others were awaiting their turn in the dock. Serious violent offenders were detained alongside the wrongly accused or those guilty only of petty public order infringement. Conditions in such places could be dire. Unequipped for long-term habitation, large cells would hold numerous prisoners without adequate bedding or sanitation. Disease and infection spread easily. Corruption amongst those who ran or were incarcerated within the prison walls was rife. Gaolers could be bribed for access to more food, alcohol and preferential treatment. Some accounts suggest that women too could be bought and sold within the prison walls, or coerced into sex by the gaolers who controlled access to provisions and visits.

The 'Bloody Code', as the eighteenth-century justice system is often referred to, began to decline in earnest by the early nineteenth century as transportation to Australia increased and social sensibilities towards violence, gender and age evolved. Theorists and officials began to accept that justice based solely on punitive measures did little to deter others from crime or to reform criminals. A whipped man tended to turn resentful towards his oppressor rather than become repentant. A hanged woman learnt nothing and those who watched her die were only deterred from getting caught. Those responsible for justice in England began to look for other ways to address the problem of crime. Industrialisation and the movement of thousands of workers into towns and cities made finding a solution to tackling and removing criminal elements in society all the more pressing.

The famous convict prisons such as Millbank and Pentonville began life in London in the early part of the nineteenth century and ushered in a fresh penal age. New prisons sought to remove criminals from society and spend years breaking their characters before releasing them back into the world as reformed and productive individuals. By the mid and later decades of the nineteenth century, as transportation came to an end, the prison system began to dominate the experience of punishment. A network of local and national institutions became a repository for the vast majority of law breakers the length and breadth of the country. From 1853, the parole system (based on the somewhat successful 'ticket of leave' system operated in Australia) was in place, discharging prisoners who passed their time peacefully and recalling those who reoffended.

Because the Victorians were amongst the first to recognise the social, cultural and developmental significance of childhood, they were the first in English history to legislate specifically for children too. This meant not only putting in place special measures for the protection of children but also providing for their punishment. In previous centuries, children of seven and eight had faced the full force of the adult law. Children of ten years old were transported and it was not unknown for children aged twelve and thirteen to face capital punishment. The Victorians not only put an end to capital punishment for those under the age of sixteen, they also created special institutions to cater for children who committed crime. These institutions allowed for the recognition of childhood as a distinct phase in a person's development, when their character and sense of morality were assumed to be forged, and kept young offenders from associating with (and learning from) the hardened adult criminals who filled convict and local prisons.

Separate penal institutions for children did not exist until 1902 with the creation of the now world-famous Borstal Prison in Kent, but institutions such as reformatory schools were created to house deviant youths. Coverage across England was sporadic, with some localities having no reformatories for girls and others like Liverpool and Coventry having multiple reformatories for young women. Girls from the age of eight to eighteen, who were convicted of crimes from prostitution to picking pockets or brawling with their neighbours, might receive a sentence of five to fourteen days in an adult prison (where hard labour or harsh conditions might 'scare them straight') followed by five or seven years in a reformatory. Young girls convicted of even just one minor offence at eleven might find themselves confined in a reformatory until they reached eighteen. The idea was simple: to catch offenders young and change their characters before they became hardened criminals. Within these institutions, often run by private funds or religious bodies, young female offenders would be given moral correction and religious education. They would be subject to strict routine and discipline and taught practical skills such as laundry work, housework and sewing, which might help them secure employment upon release. This combination of moral reformation and practical preparation was thought to help them avoid the temptation or necessity of turning again to crime.

For adult women a sentence of imprisonment meant one of two things; confinement in a local prison for a period of a few days up to two years where they might undertake corrective 'hard labour' such as picking oakum, or penal servitude from three years to life in one of England's convict prisons. Here, depending on conduct, ability and duration of sentence, they would carry out a range of domestic chores essential to the running of the prison such as laundry and cooking, or other work such as fibre pulling, sewing and knitting. For most female offenders, the end of a spell of penal servitude would entail a stay in a penal refuge. Here, still under tight controls, female convicts would be taught skills to fit them for domestic service positions upon release, although such employment was by no means assured.

The prison system was strictly regimented and highly oppressive. Alongside specialist regimes like the silent system and separate confinement, a generalised system of privileges and punishments controlled everything – what diet offenders were given, what they wore, if they could write letters and receive visitors, and what money, or 'gratuity', they could expect upon release. The message of the penal system was clear: those who obeyed would serve less time in prison and be better off when they left; those who did not obey would face physical and mental punishment. However, demanding obedience from those who have already shown nonconformity to the law, and to expect good behaviour from individuals based on the idea of future gratification, was, to put it lightly, flawed.

The time that female offenders spent in prison is often some of the best documented of their lives. The bureaucratic machine that was the Victorian state had paperwork for everything. When a woman was admitted to prison, especially convict prison, a record was taken not only of what she had done and how long she was required to be incarcerated, but also her personal history, physical description, medical history, height and weight. Records kept of the imprisoned tell us how they passed their time, from the labour they were required to carry out to the religion they followed and the prison rules they broke. Guidelines for diet and conduct let us know about prison life down to the last details of what women ate on a daily basis. The limited literacy of the women who passed through English prisons means that first-hand accounts of their experiences often come from rare cases and extraordinary offenders. However, whilst the women who wrote them were far from typical offenders they can still give us some of the most insightful descriptions of life behind bars.

Fifteen lost years

The trial of Florence Maybrick for the murder of her husband James in 1889 was one of the greatest *causes célèbres* of the Victorian Age. Florence Chandler, a young southern belle from America, had married James Maybrick, a cotton broker two decades her senior, in 1881 (see plate 3). In their unhappy eight-year marriage, the Maybricks had two children and at least two confirmed extramarital affairs. James had kept a long-term mistress for upwards of twenty years. Florence had a short-term dalliance with Alfred Brierley – one of her husband's business associates. The relationship was to change Florence's life irrevocably.

After suffering a short gastrointestinal illness in 1889, James Maybrick died in agony at the couple's home in Liverpool. Knowledge of the Maybricks' marital strife in the preceding months made James's brother suspicious of his sudden death. An autopsy on James's body found traces of the deadly poison arsenic in his body and Florence was immediately suspected of his murder.

Much contradictory evidence was provided at a hastily called trial and to this day, historians and writers remain divided as to whether Florence intentionally administered arsenic to her husband or whether his death was caused by dangerous self-medication, or even as a result of poisoning at all. What is clear to most who study the details of the case is that the evidence presented at the trial had a tendency to present Florence as cold, adulterous, licentious and heartless instead of supporting a case for criminal guilt. The prosecution sought to prove to the jury that Florence Maybrick was a woman of bad character and thus capable of murdering her husband rather than relying on the evidence that proved beyond reasonable doubt that she had, in fact, poisoned him.

The case plunged pro- and anti-Maybrick factions across the country into fierce debate. Did she do it? Could she have done it? What would happen to her now? Despite significant support for Florence both in England and America, at the close of the trial a jury wasted very little time in declaring her guilty. The judge passed the sentence of death, as was the custom in all murder cases. Florence's supporters mounted a rapid appeal and her death sentence was quickly commuted to life imprisonment. Evidence suggesting her innocence continued to be supplied to the Home Office and even Queen Victoria herself considered that the Maybrick case represented more than the fate of one woman. The imprisonment of Florence Maybrick was used to set an example to unfaithful and dissolute wives across England. The case became an exemplar of the might and power of the British justice system. To release Florence too soon would have raised many uncomfortable questions and so she was to spend the next fifteen years in prison.

Florence Maybrick may have been a far from ordinary convict, but in all likelihood, her experience of prison was very similar to that of all of the women who passed through such institutions. What we know about Florence's incarceration has left us with almost unequalled insight into a woman's experience in a Victorian convict prison. Her memoir of this time, *My Fifteen Lost Years*, was published shortly after she left prison. It gives us a rare, first-hand narrative of the terror and tedium endured by women who served at Her Majesty's pleasure.

After sentencing, Florence was transferred from Liverpool to Woking Prison, in Surrey. Once there she was placed in a prison uniform, to which, she admitted, 'the greatest stigma and disgrace is attached'. Her long hair was cut short to her neck by a matron with a pair of scissors. Florence was weighed and measured and left in the infirmary. Here, alone and frightened, her only company came from the 'raving and weeping' of an unidentified woman in an adjacent cell. The following morning, she was subjected to a medical examination and was then prepared to enter the main prison. She was taken to her own 7-foot by 4-foot cell, which contained a hammock, three shelves and a small window. Inside this room she spent nine months in solitary confinement. Florence described her daily routine:

It is six o'clock; I rise and dress in the dark; I put up my hammock and wait for breakfast; I hear the ward officer in the gallery outside. I take a tin plate and a tin mug and stand before the cell door. Presently the door opens; a brown, whole-meal, 6-ounce loaf is placed upon the plate; the tin mug is taken, and three-quarters of a pint of gruel is measured in my presence when the mug is handed back in silence and the door is closed and locked. After I have taken a few mouthfuls of bread I begin to scrub my cell. A bell rings and my door is again unlocked. No word is spoken because I know exactly what to do. I leave my cell and fall into single file, three paces in the rear of my nearest fellow convict. All of us are alike in knowing what we have to do, and we march away silently to Devine service. … Chapel over I returned directly to my cell, for I was in solitary confinement and might not enjoy the privilege of working in company with my prison companions. Work I must, but I must work alone. Needlework and knitting fall to my lot. My task for the day is handed to me, and I sit in my cell plying my needle, with the consciousness that I must not indulge in an idle moment, for an unaccomplished task means loss of marks, and loss of marks means loss of letters and visits. As chapel begins at 8.30 I am back in my cell soon after nine, and the requirement is that I shall make one shirt a day – certainly not less than five shirts a week. If I am obstinate or indolent, I shall be reported by the ward officer, and be brought to book with punishment – perhaps a reduced diet of bread and water and total confinement to my cell for twenty-four hours. If I am faint, weak or unwell, I may be excused the full performance of my task; but there must be no doubt of my inability. ... Then comes ten o'clock, and with it the governor and his escort. He inspects each cell, and if all is not as it should be the prisoner will hear of it. ... The prison bell rings again ... It is the hour for exercise, and I put on my bonnet and cape ... we march into the exercise yard. We have drawn up in line, three paces apart, and this is the form in which we tramp around the yard and take our exercise. This yard is perhaps 40 feet square, and there are thirty-five of us to expand in its 'freedom'. ... When one hour of exercise is over, in a file as before, we tramp back to our work. Confined as we are for twenty-two hours in our narrow gloomy cells, the exercise, dull as it is, is our only opportunity for a glimpse of the sky and for a taste of outdoor life, and affords our only relief from an otherwise unbearable day. At noon the midday meal ... my food is handed to me, then the door is closed and double locked. In the following two hours, having finished my meal, I can work or read. ... Work is then resumed again until five o'clock, when gruel and bread is again served, as at breakfast, with half an hour for its disposal. From that time on until seven o'clock more work, when again is heard the clang of the prison bell, and with it comes the end of our monotonous day. I take down my hammock and once more await the opening of the door. We have learned exactly what to do. With the opening of our cells we go forward, and each places her broom outside the door. ... On through the ten long weary hours of the night the night officers patrol the wards keeping watch, and through a glass peephole silently inspect us in our beds to see that nothing is amiss.

Florence labelled her months in solitary confinement 'the most cruel feature of English penal servitude'. After nine months Florence was taken from solitary and placed in the probation ward of the prison, in a bigger cell with more provisions. The routine of her days remained largely the same. Her cell door was opened for more hours of the day but she was nonetheless expected to sit and work in silence. The prison regime undergone by Florence Maybrick and thousands of other women was intended to break down an inmate's spirit, to erode their previous character and give them endless amounts of time to consider their transgressions. We know now that such systems served only to inflict psychological trauma on convicts.

After finishing her probation and surviving the separate and silent systems, Florence was moved again and undertook communal living and daily labour within the main prison. Her days were still strictly regimented but she was allowed to spend greater periods of time outside of her cell. She carried out labour in the kitchens, delivering the hot drinks and bread for morning meals. She then attended chapel before returning to work again, this time cleaning in the kitchens. The daily routine lasted approximately twelve hours with only a few hours' respite for meals. Florence wrote:

> The work was hard and rough. The combined heat of the coppers, the stove, and the steamers was overpowering especially on hot summer days; but I struggled on, doing this work preferably to some other, because the kitchen was the only place where the monotony of prison life was broken.

Throughout her memoir Florence's tedium at the prison routine is abundantly clear. She speaks of having to develop a 'mental numbness' in order to survive the unending routine. It is hard to adequately imagine the boredom and frustration felt by prisoners who found themselves repeating the same experiences over and over again, day in and day out for years. Generally, the food served to convicts each day would be the same: cocoa or tea with bread in the morning, beef or mutton stew with bread for lunch (one or two days a week might be meat free), and gruel and bread for dinner. What they wore never changed unless a prison offence saw them ordered into a canvas dress or straightjacket. Visits from approved friends and family were only allowed for prisoners who had earned the right, once every two to six months. Other than a bible, prisoners had no right to reading material or intellectual stimulation and daily visits to the chapel were the closest thing to entertainment the prison provided.

Florence served seven years in Woking prison before she was removed to Aylesbury to serve the remainder of her sentence. She was eventually released in 1904 and the following year she published the account of her time behind bars. Florence's time in prison had a great personal and practical effect on her life. Like many ex-convicts, she struggled to rebuild her former life. Her son and daughter, whom she had left as children, remained estranged to her for the rest of her life. Florence undertook a lecturing tour after her release from prison but her personal and financial life never recovered. She died impoverished and alone in America in 1941.

In Victorian England, prison time was hard time. Incarcerated women could suffer both mentally and physically at the hands of those who staffed the institutions as well as their fellow inmates. Just as prisons in present-day England struggle to police violence amongst inmates and the exploitation and abuse of vulnerable prisoners, so it was in the Victorian era. Inmates might also prove a danger to themselves. Mental illness and instability suffered by those in prisons was a largely untreated problem in the nineteenth century. Provisions for and understanding of mental health were poor and suicide attempts and incidents of self-harm were more likely to be perceived as disciplinary matters than medical crises. Many women who entered prisons had pre-existing mental health issues and others struggling to adjust to the regime could develop these conditions. Only the most basic provision was made for the safety and comfort of prisoners. In Woking, for example, 'wire netting is stretched over the lowest tier to prevent prisoners from throwing themselves over in one of those frenzies of rage and despair of which every prison has its records.'

For a few desperate women, life in prison, where their accommodation was secure, their meals were regular and their needs provided for, was more desirable than a desperate and frightening existence at the mercy of rough sleeping, unemployment and chronic want. However, for most, prison time was lonely and monotonous. Prison regimes were designed to be repressive and restrictive. They punished women by keeping them from friends and family and all the joys of liberty. Prison also sought to reform female offenders through backbreaking work and hours of silent contemplation. The relatively minor crimes that saw women lose years of their lives to the brutal regimes of these institutions makes it difficult to see the justice in their sentences, but when it came to punishment in Victorian England, was prison the best of a bad lot?

Sent away

It was long before the nineteenth century that the English legal system first began experimenting with the practice of deporting convicted men, women and children to remote locations of the empire. The first methodical attempt at ridding the motherland of her unwanted offenders was in the seventeenth century, when convicts joined free men and slaves on America's east coast. In this era transportation was not as tightly mandated by the state as it was in the eighteenth and nineteenth centuries. Convicts would be carried along with others on passenger ships headed for the New World and when the vessel made port they would be sold to wealthy merchants, businessmen and landowners as indentured servants for the term of their sentence, at great commercial gain to those who had shipped them. After such time as their sentence expired they would be free men and women once again.

Convicts arriving in America might be used as private servants, or contracted for public labour. The number and use of convicts arriving in America could impact upon the price and uses of slave labour at any given time. Although not as famous as transportation to Australia, penal transportation to America until 1776 changed forever how prisoners and punishment were perceived in the US. Even in the present day, more than a century since the end of British penal transportation and the abolition of slavery, a convict prisoner in the United States continues to hold the legal position of 'slave of the state'. The most famous account from this era of a transported female is, like so many other accounts of female offenders, a fictional one. Daniel Defoe's Moll Flanders, herself the child of a female transportee to America, was sentenced to death but was fortunately reprieved and transported to Virginia. With the turbulent period of the American Revolutionary War and the independence of America in 1776, Britain lost one of her wealthiest and most prosperous colonies as well as one of the most effective ways of getting rid of some of her criminal population.

Six years earlier, Captain James Cook and the crew of his ship HMS *Endeavour* had identified Botany Bay on the east coast of Australia as being potentially suitable for British settlement. Not only did the sun-baked continent present the opportunity of new scientific discovery and all manner of untapped potential, it also offered a convenient place for the disposal of convicts. With Australia being much further away from Britain than America there was a greatly reduced chance of offenders being able to find their way back home. In Australia, those who had broken the law in Britain could truly be placed out of sight and out of mind.

Less than twenty years later, in 1787 the First Fleet of convicts and officials set out to start the British colonisation of Australia, beginning in New South Wales. The penal policy of transporting convicts to the other side of the world continued for almost seventy years. This period saw the forced migration of more than 160,000 men, women and children from across Britain, and the resulting development of some of Australia's most thriving metropolitan areas.

The first phase of convict transportation to Australia stretched from the time when the First Fleet landed in Botany Bay up until the colony's closure to convicts in 1840. The second phase involved transportation to Van Diemen's Land (present-day Tasmania), which began in the 1820s, during the time of transportation to New South Wales, and lasted into the 1850s. By 1858, mainstream transportation of convicts to the colonies had ended. Conscious of the delicate balance between convict labour and opportunities for free migrants, Australia wanted to move towards being a convict-free nation. However, a small number of convicts were still being sent to parts of Australia up until 1868, with the last 10,000 of them landing in Freemantle, near Perth, in Western Australia. The authorities of WA were much more selective about what kind of offenders they were willing to accept. Those that they would not allow in included habitual offenders, political prisoners such as troublesome Irish radicals, and – most certainly – women. Therefore, the transportation of female offenders to Australia ended in 1858.

In the Victorian period, female offenders would be liable for the sentence of transportation if either their first offence was of a very serious nature (such as murder) or for virtually any kind of offence if it was their second (or more) appearance in the dock. In the twenty years from Queen Victoria's ascendancy to the throne to the end of transportation to Van Diemen's Land, thousands of women from across Britain were sentenced to transportation. Depending on the record of the offender and the severity of the offence, women would face a term of transportation of seven or fourteen years, or life. It was unusual for a woman to receive a long sentence of transportation, a typical sentence rarely exceeding seven years. After sentencing, an offender could wait weeks, months or even years before being boarded onto a transportation vessel, if they ever were at all. It is estimated that up to one third of offenders sentenced to transportation never left Britain's shores. Convicts sentenced to transportation were often held on hulks – crowded, dirty and deadly prison ships that lined rivers like the Thames and sat offshore at locations such as Portsmouth. The horrors of the hulks are renowned, but less well known is that they were only for the housing of male prisoners. Women awaiting such a voyage were held in separate prisons.

Like the popular commentators of the time, we might be tempted to think that transportation was a punishment reserved only for the worst female offenders – the lowly 'criminal classes' who lived entirely through the proceeds of crime or the violent and morally bankrupt. Certainly, Australia would have provided the easiest solution by which British authorities could dispose of such individuals. Transportation was seen as a harsh and final solution to deal with offenders. No bars were needed to keep convicts in Australia once they had arrived; the extreme isolation and unforgiving conditions kept the convicts in line and in place. However, whilst transportation was handed down as a standard sentence in the courtrooms of England, depending on crime and severity, there is much evidence to suggest that at the point of filling convict vessels ready to sail, there were clear desirable criteria for selection. The first of these was age. In 1812, when asked about how convicts were actually selected for a voyage, the superintendent of hulks, Mr James Capper, explained, 'We generally confine it, as nearly as possible, about two-and-forty, and not more than five-and-forty; there have been instances, where we have been imposed upon, where they wished to go, but we have brought them back.' He added that this was 'with a view to the service of the country generally; but generally speaking, they are very young that go out, from London in particular.'

Capper was not wrong and his policies outlived his tenure as superintendent. Decades later, in the Victorian period women were still transported at a remarkably young age. Betsy Simpson, aged fifteen, was transported to Van Diemen's Land aboard the *Platina* in 1837 for a term of fourteen years having stolen 48 yards of thread edging worth twenty shillings. In 1843, 14-year-old Jane Callahan was transported aboard the

Woodbridge after stealing a shawl and a tablecloth, and in 1852, 16-year-old Mary Ashdown set sail on the *Duchess of Northumberland* for a seven-year sentence after stealing a dress and petticoat.

The colonies did not just want young women. They also wanted women that were healthy and skilled so that they might survive the gruelling journey across the seas, which could last six months or more, and so they might be of use to the new colony. Domestic servants and factory workers were common occupations of the women on ships' manifests. Australia needed women that could work, reproduce and serve rather than presenting a financial and social burden to the fledgling society. The elderly and infirm were not seen to be of use in this respect. Almost all of the female offenders sent to Australia were of child-bearing age. Whilst Capper refuted that this was the specific purpose of age selection, there was an implicit hope that once these women had served their time they would choose to stay in the colony, marry, have children and form a stable foundation for Australia's future.

Throughout Van Diemen's Land and New South Wales a network of thirteen 'female factories' were used for the confinement of female convicts. After arrival, women were sent to the factories briefly while awaiting a work assignment. They could also be sent there if they were found to be pregnant while under sentence or as secondary punishment if they transgressed colony rules. The female factory was a form of punishment within a punishment. Women who were violent or disorderly in the convict system, or those who committed another offence while they served their sentence in the colony, would be sent to a factory to work under stricter rules and tighter observation. (See plate 4.) Very much like the English prison system back home, women in the factories were expected to undertake daily work. Sewing, knitting and spinning were the most common chores. Those undergoing secondary punishment could also be forced to carry out harder and more hazardous tasks.

Transportation was framed by Victorian authorities as a one-way ticket – a voyage of no return. After having served their sentences, unlike convicts released from England's prisons, transported convicts faced little prospect of returning to their former lives. After years spent thousands of miles from home in Australia's temperate climate, a convict's liberation spelt not only the end of their service to the state but a new beginning too. Many of those who chose to remain in Australia after release found new opportunities for employment, having a family and even owning land. Former convicts could build the kind of life that had been out of their grasp during their former years in England. Even for those who did want to return to England, the prospect of months at sea and the prohibitive cost of such a voyage saw them remain in Australia for the rest of their lives.

Only a minority of Australia's released convicts ever returned to England's shores. An even smaller number risked the consequences of returning from transportation while still under sentence. If captured they would face re-transportation for life or, later in the nineteenth century, a term in prison.

Susan Morris was born in London in 1813. Up until the age of sixteen, Susan lived with her grandmother, Jane, in Hoxton, in the East End. Jane worked as washerwoman, taking in items to launder for the more well-off inhabitants of the neighbourhood. This was a meagre living, but enough to keep the two women fed and housed. However, Susan suddenly left the family home in February 1829. On 27 April that year, Susan visited two of the families for whom her grandmother washed and asked for the dirty linen so that she might take it away. It was not unusual for members of a washerwoman's family to run errands on her behalf, and unaware that Susan had not been in the service of her grandmother for a number of weeks, the obliging servants happily handed over their employers' items. Visiting the household of Mr John Todd and Mr George Appold, Susan was able to take away eighty-eight items of clothing and household linen ranging from small pieces such as handkerchiefs, stockings and shirt collars, to more valuable belongings like shirts, dresses and waistcoats, and even curtains. The combined value of these items was several pounds. It is not hard to imagine that for a poor girl alone in Hoxton such easily available goods that might be sold or pawned for a large sum of easy money (more than she could ever hope to make) proved too much of a temptation to resist.

Later that same day the authorities were alerted to the offence by a member of Susan's own family. Whilst blood ties often inspired loyalty when faced with the police, those on the very cusp of destitution could little afford to lose their only source of income. If Susan was not caught and the goods not returned, Jane's business in the local area would suffer or cease altogether. Susan was apprehended in the upstairs 'dancing room' of the Salmon &

Ball pub, wearing some of the stolen property. On searching her, a key was found that opened a box she kept at her lodgings in Spitalfields. Inside was the remainder of the missing items. With such damming evidence, multiple witnesses and even her own family willing to testify against her, Susan's trial was swift. She was convicted of two separate counts of simple larceny at the Old Bailey in June 1829, and was banished to Australia for a total of fourteen years.

In contrast to others who spent months or years awaiting their sentence, within a month Susan had be selected for a convict voyage. On 10 July 1829, the ship *Lucy Davidson* set sail for New South Wales, arriving in November that year. Susan celebrated her seventeenth birthday on the voyage. With no record of conviction in Australia, or any documents of her conduct during her sentence at all, we must assume that the majority of her time in New South Wales passed without incident. Indeed, she must have worked through the convict system and obtained a good degree of freedom because in the late 1830s she was able to board a boat and return to England before her sentence had expired.

By 1838, Susan was noticeably darker in complexion after almost a decade in Australia, and living back in London. She was living with a man named Jackson, whom she had supposedly married in New Zealand. Susan was arrested in November 1838, almost nine years to the day from when she arrived in New South Wales. She was charged with illegally returning from transportation. Constable William Attfield apprehended Susan after receiving an anonymous tip-off that she was a returned convict. Susan was, to Attfield's account, greatly distressed at being apprehended. She 'cried a great deal and begged hard for me to let her go, and said she would give me all she possessed in the world if I would let her go about her business.' William Hale, the officer who had arrested her in 1829, testified that he could identify her by a unique scar by her eye, which he had remembered ever since. Although several other men testified to knowing her, and a certificate of her previous convictions was produced, there was a suggestion that Officer Hale was only quick to identify Susan because of the £20 reward that had been offered for her apprehension. Susan was found not guilty and set free. From the court, she disappeared back into London's crowded streets.

There are relatively few prosecutions evident of women, like Susan, who returned from transportation illegally. Explanations as to why this might have been the case seem fairly self-evident. Those who returned illegally were careful to disguise their identity, slipping unseen back to their lives in England. Nevertheless, it is probable that few women made the journey back to England after years abroad. Young and single women in Australia were likely to marry and build lives for themselves. Given the prospect of reasonable employment in a good climate, and the opportunity to move on successfully from their convict past, few women opted to return to the hardship and prejudice that awaited them in England.

Rarer still than those who returned while under sentence of transportation were those who built a life in Australia only to return to Britain's shores decades later when random opportunity or circumstance presented itself.

Tichborne's sister

Euphemia McCauldfield (or Mina, as she became known in Australia) was born in Ireland in 1828. Despite her unusual name, she was much like many of the other poor young women carving out a living in Dublin. In her early life Mina worked as a dressmaker. She was only distinct from most of her female convict peers in this period because she was a Protestant and able to both read and write. Typical convicts transported from Ireland to Australia tended to be poor, illiterate Catholics. Like so many men and women trying to survive at the height of the Great Famine, which cause great hardship in Ireland from 1845-52, Mina turned to crime. She was convicted of robbery in June 1847 and sentenced to seven years' transportation. (See plate 6.) She arrived in Van Diemen's Land in May 1848 after sailing on the convict ship *Anson*.

Mina spent six months in gang probation before settling into life as a third-class convict (one of the lower ranks, offering fewer privileges). Transported prisoners in Australia had much more freedom than those imprisoned in Britain. If the right conditions of their servitude were met they could be free to undertake private employment, and even to marry. In 1849, just a year after arriving, Mina married a local free man and coxswain, Francis Jury. She was eventually released on licence in 1853, after five and a half years as a convict. She had eighteen months left to serve on her sentence but was to all intents and purposes a free woman.

As long as she followed the conditions of her licence for those eighteen months and gained no further convictions, Mina was free to begin a new life. And she did just that. She and Francis were married for just under twenty years and the couple had nine children together. Originally the pair settled in Tasmania and lived in Hobart until 1863. (See plate 5.) Then the Jurys moved to Adelaide so that Francis could take up a position as an officer at the prison there. They remained in Adelaide until 1867, when Francis was accidentally shot and killed. After this time, Mina and her children moved to Melbourne as many of the extended Jury family had settled in the city and could provide support for Mina and offer employment for the older Jury children.

As a female convict, and then a free woman in Australia, Mina was largely unremarkable. Excepting the nature, perhaps, of Francis's untimely death, her story reads like those of the tens of thousands of others who were transported and went on to start life afresh in Australia. After her release, the stain of conviction seemed quite removed from Mina's life. She only became exceptional when she sailed to England in 1873 to take part in one of the most notorious legal cases of the day. Her return to the United Kingdom coincided with a return to crime and a series of events that saw Mina's name become a footnote in history.

The year after Mina was released on licence in Hobart, a capsized ship was recovered just off the Brazilian coast. There were faint rumours that survivors of the shipwreck had been collected by another ship and transported to safety in Australia. However, officially, it was assumed that all life on board had been lost. One of the passengers said to have perished aboard the ship was Roger Tichborne, the heir to a baronetcy in Hampshire. Lady Tichborne, Roger's mother, never fully gave up hope that her son had survived and in the early 1860s began placing adverts in English newspapers pleading for information on the shipwreck and survivors. By 1865 her pleas had reached further abroad, searching for news of survivors in Australia. Later that year, a man named Arthur Orton (alias Thomas Castro), from Wagga Wagga in New South Wales, declared himself to be the long-lost Tichborne heir.

It was never definitively proven that Orton was not Tichborne, but it remains highly unlikely that he was. Despite a lack of concrete evidence, after coming forward, Orton was accepted both by Lady Tichborne and a number of wealthy friends in France and England as the lost aristocrat. In 1871, an initial court case to obtain legal recognition as Tichborne collapsed and Arthur Orton was sent to prison for perjury. A criminal case against Orton began in 1873 and lasted almost a year. Both the prosecution and defence scoured the globe for witnesses that could attest to Orton's true identity.

Mina Jury came forward as a witness for the prosecution. She was, according to them, 'sister' to the defendant. In reality their connection was a distant one. Mina's brother-in-law, Captain Jury, had married Arthur Orton's sister, Elizabeth. The Ortons and the Jurys had lived for a time within the same community in Hobart, where Arthur worked as a butcher. Mina had herself known Arthur and was none too fond of him. Orton had stolen from her the sum of £14, she testified. Mina knew that his claim to be Tichborne was a fraud. Mina's role as a witness was a relatively minor one. Orton was eventually found guilty of a felony and imprisoned. The case caused a media sensation and has gone down as one of the greatest scandals of the nineteenth century.

Mina had initially been under the impression that travelling to England to take part in the case might earn her £500 or even £1,000. Yet she only ever received £18 for her troubles, plus the costs of her travel and accommodation in England while she was testifying. The Tichborne affair did not make Mina rich but it did prove a watershed in her life. Her role in the trial uprooted her from the life she had built in Australia. More importantly, the case showed Mina the world of possibilities open to those prepared to put on a convincing act. Not content with her treatment by the courts Mina did not return to Australia. She stayed in England for more than a decade and embarked upon a career of theft and fraud every bit as daring as Arthur Orton's.

The year after the Tichborne trial, in November 1874 Mina posed as a genteel lady by the name of Madam Caradena. She claimed to be on a sketching tour and rented an apartment in the Bate Hall Inn, Macclesfield. Mina was supplied by the landlady with some writing materials and shortly afterwards left the apartment to run errands. When she failed to return the next day the landlady checked 'Madam Caradena's' lodgings only to find that the apartment had been stripped of everything of value. The stolen property was recovered by the police the following afternoon, and the day after, Mina herself was captured. Rather damningly, Mina was found by police in the doorway of a pawnshop, having just pledged more stolen articles. A number of other pawn tickets were found on her; some were even stitched into her clothing for safety. Mina was taken into custody and was to be tried for a felony. As transportation to Australia had ceased, her conviction would not mean a return home, but a spell in one of England's prisons. First, she was remanded in Macclesfield Gaol for a week.

The evening before her trial, when the lock-up keeper came into her cell with her supper, Mina implored him to check under her bed as she had seen a rat. As the obliging gaoler knelt down, Mina rushed past him and out of the cell, bolting it from the outside. With the guard trapped inside Mina was free to make good her escape from the gaol. She was recaptured four days later at Leek, almost 15 miles away. The following week Mina was given six months' imprisonment.

Mina was released from prison in May 1875 and was immediately apprehended in Cheshire for another offence. She had stolen a pair of gold eyeglasses and pawned them in Manchester. In court, Mina cross-examined the witnesses at considerable length and stated, 'I want to know what the newspapers will say about me. I am in a strange country and want justice done to me.' An infuriated judge was forced to interject: 'Now listen to me, Mrs Jury, I can't stay here all day and listen to you.' He remanded her for trial in July. At her trial, indicating a level of inflated self-importance, Mina recounted for the jury at length her involvement in the Tichborne trial. It did little to help her case and she was sentenced to three months' hard labour.

In June the following year, Mina appeared in London at the Old Bailey. She was charged with stealing knives and a bag of surgical instruments with a combined value of £15. Mina had visited the house of a surgeon in Hammersmith and asked for an appointment. The surgeon was out and Mina was left to wait for him in a consulting room. She waited patiently for some time and then left suddenly. In the coming days the knives and surgical bag were missed. Mina pledged all of the items to a pawnbroker under an alias of Ann Brown but the items were traced back to her. Mina was found guilty of this offence and remained in court to face another similar charge for stealing a rug from a surgeon in Peckham. For this, she was found not guilty. Mina then faced a third charge of stealing surgical instruments from a doctor in Greenwich. In total, there were 'more than a dozen similar cases' against Mina, who was sentenced on this occasion to seven years of penal servitude.

After her release from prison in 1881, Mina's tactics changed. She was no longer interested in the effort of small-scale thefts and the danger of pledging stolen items at the pawnbroker. Instead, she turned her attention to the more lucrative proceeds of fraud. In the early 1880s, using the rather extravagant name of Ada Menne Sempriere, Mina had been appealing to various 'noble and gentlemen' for charitable funds, and making a not insubstantial living from them. A newspaper reported:

> One of her victims was His Royal Highness the Duke of Edinburgh, from whom she obtained the sum of £15 on the representation that she was known to His Royal Highness at Adelaide, in the year 1867, as Miss Gordon, daughter of the late Colonel Gordon and niece of Sir Dominic Daly, Governor of Adelaide.

The duke had the case recommended to him by a friend, the Earl of Kilmorey, who was deeply moved by 'Ada's' predicament and wholly convinced by the details she produced of the royal visit to Adelaide. Mina had been present in Adelaide at the time of the royal visit; it was the year in which her husband Francis was shot dead. Mina would not have been considered important enough to meet with royalty, but had enough memories of the visit to create an elaborate and believable narrative. She further claimed that she had only recently arrived in England from Alexandria, where she had been travelling with her husband and young son. While in Alexandria, she said, her husband and son had been killed by 'Arabs' and she herself had barely escaped with her life. It was a story told well enough to fool some of the most wealthy and powerful people in the country. Almost unbelievably for a case of fraud by a repeat offender and paroled convict, Mina was sentenced to only six months' imprisonment with hard labour for the crime.

Mina's final conviction took place in 1885, a year after the Tichborne claimant, Arthur Orton, was released from his own lengthy prison sentence.

During this year Mina was implicated in several crimes, perpetrated as far apart as Stoke-on-Trent and London. She had failed to report to police under the terms of her licence for parole. She had stolen money and items from a lodging house and had again been presenting herself to influential gentlemen as a well-connected woman in need of assistance. Amongst them were the mayor of Stoke-on-Trent and a lodge of freemasons. Again, she was found guilty of obtaining 'various sums of money by fraud'. As Mina was sentenced to another five years of penal servitude Arthur Orton was touring the country and presenting lectures in crowded venues about his experiences and trial. In several places, he lectured on Mina's bad character and subsequent criminal activity. A further five years in an English convict prison was more than enough for Mina, who afterwards returned to Australia and did not come to the attention of the courts again. It seems that life as a former convict in Australia was an easier and more law-abiding one for Mina than her exploits in England.

The physical and psychological upheaval suffered by convicts forcefully sent to Australia make it difficult now to think of transportation as being anything other than a cruel and harsh punishment. Women sent to New South Wales and Van Diemen's Land were, in many cases, ripped from their families, friends and everything familiar. It is hard to say with any certainty that life as a convict in Australia was any happier than life inside an English convict prison. Surely, the experience of years as a captive of the state was not to be relished in either hemisphere. However, from what we know of the chances of women released on licence and eventually set at liberty it seems that reform and a life lived free of the stain of former conviction may well have been easier overseas. Brutal or not, transportation without doubt provided a more appealing punishment than the fate that awaited England's most serious female offenders on their home soil.

Launched into eternity

Before the modern prison system or transportation across the seas there was a system of justice that has remained iconic even into the twenty-first century: the Bloody Code of the eighteenth century has become a legend of English history. Prior to the nineteenth century, those found guilty of crimes faced a range of corporal and capital punishments. Sentences might include whippings – either inside a gaol or in public. For women there might be the additional humiliation of being stripped to the waist. Earlier decades had seen brandings and facial mutilation to mark out thieves or those who perjured themselves. There was also the grim spectre of the pillory (stocks), in which the guilty party would be forced to stand or sit for days at a time while the public watched their humiliation and pelted them with insults and rotting produce, stones or excrement. 'Mother' Elizabeth Needham, one of London's most famous eighteenth-century brothel keepers (and inspiration for William Hogarth's famous *A Harlot's Progress* etchings), died in 1731 after enduring three days in the pillory.

The most famous and feared part of the Bloody Code was, of course, the death penalty. Execution gallows existed in most towns and cities but the most notorious site of pre-Victorian execution is Tyburn, in London. Crowds of avid spectators would gather to hear the last words and watch the final moments of a convict's life at the gallows. Prior to the nineteenth century, there were an astonishing number of 'capital crimes' that could lead to the death sentence – anything from pickpocketing to poaching or rape could earn an offender's execution. Whilst many death sentences were reprieved, the spectre of the hangman's noose was a constant in English justice at this time.

The effect of the Bloody Code was thought to be twofold. Firstly, physical consequences for breaking the law quite clearly had a punitive effect. Such corporal punishments were supposed to be unpleasant to undergo and thus would exact revenge on offenders for their transgressions. Secondly, punishments were also hoped to have a deterrent effect. The idea was that after an unpleasant experience such as whipping or the pillory an offender would not risk a repeat of the treatment by committing another crime. In reality, this approach was only minimally effective. Not only were offenders brutalised by physical punishments but there was also no attempt to help them to reform or address the circumstances that caused their offending. Corporal and capital punishments were also supposed to deter through fear those who saw them carried out or heard about them. In the case of hanging, it was obvious that the executed would learn nothing from the experience but it was assumed that the horrified crowd who watched the spectacle would be so traumatised that they would be put off from committing crime lest they suffer the same fate, although there is no evidence to suggest that this was actually effective.

As the eighteenth century moved into the nineteenth and the Victorian era dawned, the same social sensibilities that recognised the special status of children and demanded different roles for men and for women also called for a more rational, civilised and progressive society. Violent and brutalising punishments gave way to methods that allowed for moral education and reform. Corporal punishment was replaced by fines, incarceration and hard labour and only the most serious crimes carried the death sentence.

By the middle of the nineteenth century, only the most notorious cases of murder warranted the death sentence for women. The gender ideals that governed almost every other aspect of Victorian society played a role in protecting many convicted women from the gallows. The same cultural norms that held women as weak, corruptible and in need of protection could not easily be overridden to make a case for female execution. A large proportion of women initially sentenced to death for their crimes were eventually granted a reprieve and given instead the sentence of life imprisonment. Overwhelmingly, those women on whom capital punishment was carried out were high profile cases in which the convict had murdered multiple victims. Also, these cases reflected a strong class dynamic. If a woman could be proved in some way to still conform to the expectations of her gender, her life would be spared. A death sentence could be overturned even in the most serious of cases if a Victorian lady looked the part, represented herself well, gained public sympathy or had a powerful advocate speak on her behalf. Working-class women who committed murder (or more than one murder) were rarely so lucky. In general, though, hangings of women in the Victorian period were the exception rather than the rule. As the *Sheffield Telegraph* noted in 1890, there was a 'strong public feeling which exists against hanging women. Again and again women have been sentenced at the Old Bailey and again and again they have been reprieved.' There were just five women hanged at Newgate from 1840 to 1890 – an average of just one per decade.

Whilst capital punishment continued well into the twentieth century (with Ruth Ellis becoming the last woman to be hanged in the United Kingdom in 1955), the spectacle of public execution became distasteful to the Victorians almost a century before. In addition, public hangings were considered to pose a serious threat to public order as they encouraged crowds, drinking and crime. From 1868, hangings took place in private, with the condemned taking their final moments behind prison walls. The public fascination with hangings, and the lust for detailed descriptions of a convict's last moments, changed little from the days of public execution. The practice of selling pamphlets and souvenirs to commemorate executions, as well as detailed newspaper reports of the scenes at the gallows, remained popular throughout the period.

From Newgate's dark beam

The execution of serial murderer Catherine Wilson in 1862 was the first hanging at Newgate in more than a decade. Catherine's conviction for multiple poisonings was one of the best-covered cases of female offending in Victorian England. Newspapers and printers catered to an outraged public, offering blow-by-blow accounts of her trials, updates on her imprisonment and meticulous coverage of her punishment right up until her final moments (see plate 7).

In June 1862, Catherine was tried at the Old Bailey under the alias of Constance Wilson for two counts of having 'feloniously administered' an ounce of sulphuric acid to her employer, Sarah Carnell, with intent to murder her.

Catherine and Sarah had known each other for five years, although Sarah knew Catherine as 'Mrs Taylor'. The pair had been in the practice of paying each other social visits. After Sarah separated from her husband, Catherine's visits to her became more frequent. Unbeknown to Sarah, her husband was now living with Catherine. In February, when Catherine was visiting Sarah, Sarah became very ill. Catherine went for medicine and stayed with Sarah into the evening so that she might nurse her. That night she gave to Sarah a 'black draught', which when poured into a glass began to heat it. Catherine encouraged Sarah to drink, but as she took a sip the liquid burned her mouth and she was forced to spit it out onto the bed. The spillage eventually burned a hole through the sheet. Several experts testified that the burns caused to Sarah's mouth and items that the liquid had touched were caused by sulphuric acid. Yet, too much conflicting and circumstantial evidence saw Catherine walk free after the jury found her not guilty.

The very next day, Catherine Wilson was arrested again and forced to appear at Lambeth Police Court on the charge of having caused the death of another woman, Mrs Ann Atkinson, by arsenic poisoning. Ann, a 55-year-old dressmaker from Westmorland, travelled to London in October 1860 for the purpose of purchasing material. She went straight from Euston Station to the house where Catherine was living as wife to a Mr Taylor. Catherine and Ann had known each other for about seven years. By all accounts, Ann had been in good health but after a light dinner, prepared for her by Catherine, she began to suffer from 'burning in the chest' and vomiting. Ann went up to bed and was nursed in the days afterwards by Catherine, who conscientiously brought her beef tea and barley water. Ann never recovered and died days after her initial attack of illness.

No foul play was suspected at the time and Ann's body was taken back to Westmorland for burial. The suspicions of the Atkinson family were only aroused two years later, in April 1862, when they saw a report in the paper concerning Catherine Wilson and the poisoning of Sarah Carnell. The Atkinson family took what evidence they had to the police. An application was made to exhume Ann Atkinson's remains and an examination proved traces of arsenic to be present in her body. A criminal case was brought against Catherine and it was further proved that she had stolen some money that Ann carried with her to London for business back in 1860.

The Atkinson application brought to light a third case, this time from Boston, Lincolnshire. Years prior to the murder of Ann Atkinson, Catherine Wilson had been living as the housekeeper of a retired master mariner named Peter Mawer. In 1854 he had been convinced by Catherine to alter his will in her favour. Mawer made arrangements to the effect that if he should die Catherine would receive a living of £80 a year from his estate. Shortly afterwards, Mawer became unexpectedly ill and died, apparently of natural causes. When his body was exhumed eight years later, in the light of Catherine's growing notoriety, an inquest showed that 'the symptoms previous to death were those of poisoning by arsenic'. A nurse who had assisted Mawer when he was ill gave evidence that he was always worse in the evenings after his meal and tea were prepared for him by Catherine.

Although it was never possible to retrieve enough physical evidence from Mawer after his body was exhumed, rumours began to swell about the multiple places in which Catherine Wilson had acted as friend, servant or guest and her acquaintances had died. One newspaper wrote:

> It is possible that these cases may fail in the legal proof, but they prove this fact – that wherever this woman introduced herself as a friend or a sister of mercy she proved a messenger of death. In every instance in which she succeeded in getting into the household death occurred in a few days. The symptoms being always the same, and in every instance a considerable sum of money mysteriously disappeared.

For almost a decade up until July 1862, Catherine's luck had been incredible. She had been a key figure in the death of several people but through strategic name changes (she was known as Catherine Wilson, Constance Wilson and Catherine Taylor) and relocation from place to place, none of the deaths had been connected together. The cumulative case against her was made all the stronger for the fact that the individual cases were so similar to each other. Catherine had been formulaic in her endeavours. Despite there being evidence enough to tie her to at least three other murders, no conviction materialised for the deaths of Sarah Carnell, Ann Atkinson or Peter Mawer.

Catherine reappeared the following month at Lambeth Police Court, charged with another murder. This time the victim was a Mrs Maria Soames and the crime dated back to October 1856, just two years after she had poisoned Peter Mawer. Catherine had been working as a maid for Mrs Soames in London. A doctor testified that Mrs Soames had usually been in good health; she had been a strong woman with a healthy constitution. In 1856 she had seemed to suffer from an attack of cholera. The doctor attested that he had done his best to treat her. When Mrs Soames had deteriorated and died not long after the doctor's visit the shocked physician refused to issue a death certificate without a post-mortem examination. Early indications of the examination suggested that Mrs Soames had ingested poison. The doctor left the materials for testing with an assistant who had since left the country and had never returned for the results of the analysis. The attention Catherine had gained in the press when accused of other murders re-opened interest in the case.

With a new investigation into the death of Maria Soames, Catherine Wilson's luck ran out. A trial for murder began at the Old Bailey in September 1862. The prosecution asserted that in October of 1856 Mrs Soames had taken to her bed complaining of 'a sickness and a great pain in her body and head'. During the illness, Catherine, a seemingly devoted long-term friend, cared for Mrs Soames. Witnesses who saw the two women together noted that 'she seemed very attentive ... giving her what she required in the way of medicine and aliment.' Catherine had, in reality, been acting as gatekeeper, determining who could and who could not see Mrs Soames during her illness. She also ensured that all medicine for Mrs Soames was brought to her first. She was also the one to administer it. Mrs Soames died a day after becoming ill.

In the lead-up to Mrs Soames's death, Catherine had borrowed almost £100 from her, on one pretence or another. As Mrs Soames approached death Catherine began to fabricate a story about the missing money for Mrs Soames's friends and family. She alleged that Mrs Soames had lent it to a man whom she thought had intended to marry her but had since disappeared without a trace. Although a post-mortem was carried out, Catherine had used a poison derived from the colchicum flower, which at that time was difficult to trace scientifically. A bottle of the poison was found amongst Catherine's belongings, and she admitted that she had been in the 'habit' of administering to the man with whom she was cohabiting.

The jury took two hours to return a guilty verdict. The judge applauded them for their findings and suggested that if they had pronounced Catherine not guilty he would have ensured that a new trial for the murder of Ann Atkinson would have immediately begun. With little hesitation, Catherine was sentenced to death. There was no recommendation for mercy. In fact, at the close of the trial the presiding judge 'thought it right that the jury and the public should know what sort of person it was that had at length been reached by the avenging arm of the law', and proceeded to describe her previous offences – even those that had not been proved by a court. As far as the authorities knew, Mawer had been Catherine's first victim, in October 1854. Catherine then moved to London in hope of wealthier targets. In 1855, she lived with a Mr Dixon, as a lodger in a house owned by Mrs Soames. In July of 1856, Dixon died after a vomiting sickness. Months later,

Mrs Soames herself was also dead. In 1859, Wilson moved in with a widow named Mrs Jackson and Catherine convinced her to part with more than £100 of her dead husband's money. Mrs Jackson died within a week and no trace of the money or Catherine was found. In 1860, Catherine Wilson was instrumental in the last days of Ann Atkinson's life. The mysterious Mr Taylor, with whom Wilson had been living, fell ill the following year but, suspecting what had happened, managed to access the required remedies and survived. The following year, Catherine had attempted to kill Sarah Carnell. Whilst she had been acquitted of the crime, recent evidence would seem to suggest that she was almost certainly guilty. What Catherine did from the years 1856 to 1859 is a mystery. There remains a very real possibility that her unknown victims number in the dozens.

In a quite unusual turn of events, Catherine was told that the court 'could not hold out to her any hope of commutation of the death sentence.' Catherine applied directly to the Queen for clemency. She argued that she was deaf and had been unable to follow the evidence given at her trial, that she was too 'want of means' to be able to afford adequate defence for herself and, lastly, that she had little medical knowledge that would have allowed her to perpetrate the crime in question. In a letter that talked of duty, service and mercy, Catherine also argued that in the six years from the time of Mrs Soames's death to the trial, friends and family related to Maria Soames had created a fictionalised account of her behaviour. Evidently, the state was unmoved by Catherine's pleas and she received no reprieve. She was told she would face the gallows.

Catherine Wilson's merciless exploitation of the weak and vulnerable for financial gain left little room for doubt, in the public mind, that she was deserving of the most severe punishment. Her crimes also played upon the very middle-class fears of the sneaking female poisoner: a villain that usually dwelled within the victim's own home and struck without suspicion – a servant, a friend or a nurse. There were very few who sought for Catherine to be rescued from her fate. It was an eager public crowd that gathered at Newgate Prison to jeer Catherine and catch a glimpse of her execution, as the following report dramatically explained:

Thousands of persons assembled long before daylight around the dreary prison walls, all anxiously awaiting daylight and the striking of that hour – the hour at which so many ill-fated mortals have been launched from Newgate's dark beam into eternity – when the object of their morbid curiosities was to make her entrance and her exit.

Never do people take their stand and watch the still hours of the night – cold and wet – pass by as they do when in front of the gallows. It would be well if the indomitable perseverance exhibited by people getting a 'good sight' of the gallows and the patience with which they wait the hour of 'exhibition' were turned to better account.

The night passed away: the morning came and at the appointed hour the promised 'sight', Calcraft, the hangman, and Catherine Wilson, the poisoner, accompanied by the Rev Chaplain, the Governor of Newgate, and Sheriffs of Middlesex made their appearance at the gallows, and the tragedy commenced. The Ordinary read prayers, and Calcraft face to face with the wretched woman, adjusted the rope round her neck and disappeared. In an instant afterwards while she cried 'Lord have mercy on me!' and the crowd yelled, the drop fell, and Catherine Wilson after a few struggles was dead. Died without the pity of even the sensitive and sympathetic. The lifeless body dangled to and fro in the air, and the crowd dispersed feeling that the old gallows for once, at least, had been just.

Catherine Wilson's hanging was the first to take place at Newgate since that of Harriet Parker, a woman convicted of murdering the two children of her lover in 1848. After a long fourteen-year wait, Catherine's execution provided a grizzly exhibition for a new generation of spectators. The infrequency with which female executions took place meant that when they did occur accounts of the event were rapaciously devoured by the public. By the time women such as Catherine stepped upon the gallows there was almost always a common sense of the details of the case: the woman's legal guilt and the utter righteousness of the punishment she was about to receive.

Special pamphlets and broadsides gave the most extensive coverage of executions. These documents contained descriptions and original poems or songs to mark the occasions. Newspapers too seized the opportunity to give their readers the salacious details of a woman's death that did not have to be treated with the delicacy of a tragedy.

The following song was included by a printer from Spitalfields on a 'broadside' souvenir poster, sold to the public to commemorate Catherine Wilson's execution:

Time: Ave Maria

My time is come, my race is run,
My time is come to die:
Oh such a dreadful death I meet,
Upon the gallows high
The cursed name of Poisoner
I carry to my grave;
What I would give one hour to live –
But my life I cannot save

Since my sentence has been fixed
On my bed I cannot rest
Horrid visions haunt my pillow
My mind is sore distress'd:
A warning voice rings in my ear,
This is the well known cry:
Catherine Wilson now prepare for death
Upon the gallows high

Such deeds I did commit in life,
For the sake of worldly gain:
I have seen my victims lay and die
In anguish and in pain
I gave, as they thought, friendship's cup
And good news to them did bring.
Poor souls, they little thought
That it was the adder's sting

This is my last night on the earth,
Pray for my soul to save
In the short space of time that's given
For I shall find a murderer's grave.
No stone will mark the spot,
My body burnt with lime:
Oh what a death for a woman to die,
That is scarcely in her prime.

The officers will awaken me,
Just before the final hour:
The hangman stands with rope in hand,
By the law he is empower'd.
The dull sound of the workmens' hammers
Ascends unto the sky
Erecting of the fatal place
For the poisoner to die.

In my last hours of sleep I dreamt I saw
My victims around my bed
Interceding for my soul above,
For I must meet my maker in dread.
With Palmer and others I must appear
Upon the judgement day.
Prepare to die for in one hour
You are a mass of lifeless clay.

The hangman awaits to pinion me –
The procession moves along –
The dead bell strikes out a dreadful peel –
Hark! I hear the busy throng.
The solitude will gaze on me
As they did on those before,
The signal given – the bolt is drawn –
Catherine Wilson is no more.

Chorus
Catherine Wilson thus did die,
A dreadful death upon the gallows high.

As one of England's most notorious female poisoners, Catherine's fate did not end with her death. It was the lot of women like Catherine Wilson to provide cautionary tales and an example to the women of England. The message was clear: those who committed the ultimate transgression would pay the ultimate price. The effective nature of the reporting of executions and the immortalisation of those who faced the gallows is evident even today. The names and stories of women like Mary Ann Cotton and Amelia Dyer still rear their ugly heads when modern female murderers grace the news.

From locking women up for years on end and assigning them menial and backbreaking labour, to sending them thousands of miles across the seas to a strange land or taking from them their very lives, it is not difficult to argue that the Victorian penal system was tough on offenders. Women who fell afoul of the law faced severe punishments. But there is little evidence to suggest that a system tough on criminals was by default tough on crime. It is true enough that female killers never reoffended after facing the gallows but then again they never worked, formed families or did anything else either. Transportation certainly cleared criminal women from the streets of England, often permanently, but whether it stopped crime or merely displaced it is another matter. Those sent to English prisons, to be broken down and reformed in a more moral and industrious mould, were invariably damaged. What characterised the Victorian prison system more than anything else was a revolving door of crime that saw as many as nine out of ten of those released returning to prison after reoffending. Women released from prisons found themselves tarnished almost indefinitely by the label of criminality that followed them home from institutions. They were at the bottom of the social heap in a society that frequently told women that even death could be preferable to dishonour and disgrace. All of this was counterproductive to rehabilitation and preventing female offending in the first place.

Chapter 2

Got to Pick a Pocket or Two?

Crimes of Property

Gruesome murders and fearful attacks have always made good stories for those who want to sell papers. Much like in the modern press, the Victorians savoured the opportunity to report on crimes that were dark and frightening. Generally, monstrous violence makes a much better headline than a story of a pair of boots stolen from a shop. However, property crimes like theft, burglary and robbery were (and still are) far more common than crimes of violence. The tendency of newspaper reports in the nineteenth century to focus on murders, drunkenness and debauchery left Victorian readers with an unrealistic perception of how common different kinds of crime were. Those braving the streets of England's cities after dark did not always realise that they were far more likely to lose their wallets and jewellery than their lives. The plethora of reports about danger and violence in the Victorian period have also coloured our own understanding of crime at this time. After all, slit throats and child murder still pique more interest than black-market trading or burglary. We do have some familiar tales of property crime in this era, though. You can hardly think of the name Dickens without imagining the Artful Dodger and a gang of ragged pickpockets. The scenario of a finely dressed lady shoplifter stowing teacups amongst her petticoats also has a distinctly Victorian feel to it. Yet the property crime that took place in Victorian England was more complex than cheeky child thieves and kleptomaniacs.

Women in the Victorian era were capable of carrying out any of the crimes of theft and fraud that their male counterparts undertook. Women could be pickpockets and shoplifters, but they could also be highway robbers, fencers of stolen goods or fraudsters. For most female offenders the remit of property crime extended to far more creative endeavours than history has remembered. Female thieves and tricksters in this period had to be inventive, highly adaptable and, in most cases, absolutely ruthless. Female property offenders were part of a racket of illicit buying and selling that was only half-visible to the rest of society. Most lived an existence where anything that came readily to hand had a price too valuable to pass up. As such, the world of female property crime was one in which anything could be obtained if only one knew who to ask, where stolen goods could always find a new owner, victims could be found around every corner and money could literally be made. Anyone willing to take what didn't belong to them could be a property offender but, like almost every other kind of crime in England at the time, it was the poor and desperate who most often turned to theft and found themselves at the mercy of the courts because of it. Property crime presented a final option to those in desperate circumstances and with nothing left to lose. It might also be a lucrative alternative to the menial and poor wages women could expect to obtain by honest means.

The nature of property crime was as diverse as the women who committed it and the circumstances that drove them to steal. Some women only resorted to theft when they were at their most desperate; others made a career from stealing that lasted decades. Some women specialised in particular kinds of property crime and would hone and practice their skills in the trade. Other women might resort to several different types of property crime over a lifetime, taking opportunities to steal or defraud as they presented themselves.

The sheer number of ways that Victorian women found to make money illegally means that compiling a comprehensive list of offences is virtually impossible. Instead, this chapter examines some of the most intriguing and common property offences in which women were involved. From child stripping, thieving serving girls and famed conwomen to the merciless predators who drugged their victims, their stories are those of desperation, cunning and ambition that have been largely forgotten in favour of more familiar histories of light-fingered ladies.

Heartless conduct

Child strippers were a well-known phenomenon in the Victorian period. As the name suggests, this crime involved the theft of children's clothes not from shops or private homes, but from the bodies of unwitting children themselves. Whilst young men also occasionally appeared in court charged with this crime, child-stripping was an overwhelmingly female offence. Described by the *Northampton Mercury* as 'heartless conduct', this offence saw women take advantage of the 'simplicity and credulity of childhood to accomplish their nefarious purposes'.

Unlike the twenty-first century, in which it seems inconceivable that children as young as three would be sent to a shop to settle a bill or left to play alone in busy city streets, unaccompanied children in Victorian towns and cities were far from rare. Children visited friends or relatives with baskets packed by busy parents. They went on errands alone or with siblings. When mothers wanted peace and quiet (or more likely the opportunity to get on with a gruelling round of domestic work) children could be sent to roam the neighbourhood streets until they were summoned in again.

Any occasion that saw a child outside of adult supervision was an opportunity for a child-stripper to strike. A woman much like any other would approach a single child, or even two or three if they were young enough, and lure them away to a deserted location or dark alleyway. This might be achieved with the promise of sweets or money if they obediently followed or otherwise by the woman introducing herself as a friend of the child's parent and suggesting that their mother or father had given instructions for them to come at once. Once away from prying eyes the offender would convince or coerce the child to strip down to only the most minimal of clothing before making away with whatever items she could get. Typically easy items for child-strippers to obtain and sell on or pawn were boots, shawls and coats, but others went further and took dresses, trousers and undergarments too. There were slight variations in what might be taken by child strippers. Sometimes the object they desired was not clothing but jewellery a child might have, or a valuable bundle or basket being taken on an errand. However, the tactics used by those who stole from children in this way varied little; obtain a child's confidence, get them alone and take away whatever you could. The child was left confused and distressed (and often scantily clad), and having to find their own way home. By the time the child reached assistance the offender could be long gone. Even with relatively quick rescue children did not make particularly good witnesses, especially the very young, and identification of an offender based on a child's testimony alone could be difficult.

Victims of child-stripping could be any age up to about ten, when they became too large to remonstrate with and too wise to be caught off guard. Children from the ages of three to six years old were those most often targeted. Children of this age group were just old enough to be left outside their houses unsupervised, or sent on simple errands for their parents in the local area, but also young enough to trust strangers and defer to the instruction of adults or older children without much question. After the age of ten children were not only less pliable but began to be similar in age to the youngest offenders carrying out child-stripping.

Child-strippers were described rather unfavourably by famed social investigator Henry Mayhew as 'old debauched drunken hags' in an article for the *Morning Chronicle* that later became part of the collection 'London Labour and the London Poor'. However, those who worked as child-strippers could prove to be anything but. Women of any age could perpetrate this crime as it relied not on physical dexterity or convincing interaction with other adults but simply gaining a child's trust. The ease with which this offence might be perpetrated meant that it was not unusual for child-strippers to be amongst the youngest of female offenders in Victorian England. Young women were ideally placed to carry out this crime as they attracted minimal attention. Older siblings squabbling with younger children or forcefully pulling along a younger child was commonplace in the streets of England where older siblings were so often charged with keeping the younger in line. As a result, some of the female offenders brought to court on charges of child-stripping were little more than children themselves.

The *Liverpool Daily Post* reported in 1860:

A girl, named Agnes Brown, about nine years old, who is an instrument in the hands of vile relatives for the purpose of thieving, was charged with stripping children of their clothes, beads, &c. On Thursday she was seen to take the clothes of a little girl ... and was given into custody.

Agnes was identified by a child of three years old – too young to even officially be called to the witness box.

In 1890 at Leamington Police Court a girl named Ellen Ward, aged ten years, was charged with child-stripping. It was stated that 'she enticed smaller children to herself to retired spots, and having stripped them of their clothes, decamped. She afterwards sold the articles for small sums,' around two pence each. This too may have been an offence carried out at the behest of older relatives to contribute the sums to the family coffers.

Young girls also carried out child-stripping for more frivolous purposes. A few pence made from a child's shawl could provide other children and young adults with a disposable income to spend on sweets, treats and entertainments that poverty at home denied them. In Salford in 1865, 11-year-old Margaret Brownhead was charged with stripping three children in the street. With the promise of sweets and treats they were enticed to part with their capes and shawls, which were then exchanged for cash at the local pawn shop. A sign of her age, Margaret spent her ill-gotten gains on sweets. Alice Easten and Fanny Hopper, aged eleven and nine respectively, were charged in the North East of England after stripping a number of children in 1867, selling their wares for a few pence at a time. Their motive was to obtain funds for admission to Waxy Doodles, which the *Sunderland Echo* described as 'a low penny gaff'. Likewise, Jessie Peebles, a 15-year-old from London who by all accounts had a stable and very respectable home life, was convicted in 1879 of three counts of child-stripping and also for stealing clothes from a washing line. The motive ascertained was that Jessie wanted to spend the money on purchasing sweetmeats, which she did not dare take back to her house. For what the magistrate termed 'one of the worst offences' Jessie spent twenty days in an adult gaol and then a further five years in a reformatory.

Child-stripping presented such an easy way to raise funds that the youngest offenders may not have initially recognised the severity of their actions. This offence could act as a gateway to establishing young women a steady income through theft. One such case, involving an unnamed woman from the North West of England, was reported by the *Liverpool Mercury* in 1880:

For the past two or three months, some excitement has been felt in Bootle owing to the frequency of robberies from children, both in the borough and in Seaforth, Waterloo, Walton, Everton, Kirkdale, Wavertree, Fairfield and in different parts of Liverpool. The children were robbed of money, or groceries, and in every instance their boots. The thefts were traced to a young woman who appeared in different dresses to avoid recognition, and never in the same neighbourhood on two consecutive days. The police were detailed to extra duty in order to effect her capture, but altogether without success until the other morning when an ex-constable of the county force saw a strange female talking to a child outside Christ Church Schools, Bootle. Knowing the child well and knowing the female was in no way related to it, he watched her and saw her lead the little one away through a number of back entries to a field at the back of the prison at Walton.

A constable was sent for and immediately went in search of the woman, initially without success. After he made further enquiries, he traced her to a local jam works in Bootle, where she had gone looking for employment. When apprehended and taken to the police station she made a full admission 'that she was the author of a great number of robberies from children in Liverpool and its suburbs.' The woman was reported to live in a disreputable part of Liverpool, and that her first conviction for felony had been at the age of just eleven. Since that age she had been found to have pursued 'a uniform career of crime' by stripping children. She had been in and out of prison serving various sentences and, at the time of this latest apprehension, had only just finished serving a seven-year sentence of penal servitude for child-stripping. She looked set to serve another term of the same now she had been apprehended again.

Older women too worked as child-strippers. These women probably constituted the greatest number of thieves of this type. Older child-strippers tended to be more experienced, more cunning and more cautious in their activities. Experienced child-strippers became better at varying their routine and also at evading detection. Their sprees tended to be longer and their hauls much greater than those of the young women that stole for sweets. In 1868, Ann Quinn, a Liverpudlian woman, was charged with stripping a 3-year-old of her dress, petticoat and pinafore. The child had wandered home virtually naked. After identifying Ann, the mother of her victim had followed her a few days later and gave her into police custody. Ann's residence was searched and found to contain sixteen children's hats, twenty pairs of stockings, three pairs of children's boots and three dresses, as well as other items. There were also twenty pawn tickets relating to children's items. The evidence suggested that Ann Quinn was a professional child-stripper. She was clearly well practised and had been in business for some time. In all likelihood she had been performing multiple strippings each day.

Jane Evans, a child-stripper from Manchester, was brought up in court on twenty-six simultaneous charges of child-stripping. Her methods were much the same as those of any other practitioner. One interesting detail from the case was noted by the newspaper: when working at luring children away from safety to conduct the crime, Jane was 'very respectably dressed', yet when she appeared in the dock after her arrest she wore a 'dirty, thin garment'. It appeared that Jane dressed up as a middle-class lady to commit her crimes. By playing the icon of motherly and domestic duty she found that others would trust her implicitly, assuming she was an exemplar of feminine goodness. The idealised vision of the saintly middle-class wife and mother was far removed from the everyday experiences of working women but some, like Jane Evans, found there was no better character to play when trying to win the trust of child.

In the popular imagination the child-stripper was a sinister character. Somewhere between thief and child snatcher, she lurked unidentifiably in plain sight ready to exploit defenceless babes. This offence caused distress to fearful families and to the disorientated children who were made victims. Surprisingly, though, child-stripping was actually one of the property offences where victims were not subject to physical harm. Physical interference with a stripping victim was minimal. Young children were so easy to manipulate and so willing to obey that violence was just not necessary. Verbal threats, or violence towards the victims is almost uniformly missing from accounts of child-stripping.

In the extremely rare cases where violence did befall children something labelled child-stripping could in reality be a different kind of crime made to look like a robbery. In Liverpool in the early 1890s a report surfaced of a little girl, just shy of four years old, who had been found dead in a courtyard, suffocated in a public toilet. It was noted that her boots and earrings were missing and it was supposed that a gang of child-strippers had been interrupted mid-crime and disposed of the child in this manner to stifle her cries. If this was so then this case would be an exception to the usual manner of child-stripping. The theft of jewellery and boots were perhaps an afterthought in what was primarily a violent attack on a child, or perhaps they were the actions of chancing thieves rather than established child-strippers. Clothing was more often a target of child-strippers than jewellery. Child-strippers primarily worked alone rather than in groups. In most cases if a child made a noise it was easier for a child-stripper to move on to another victim than to commit a murder. The culprits and details of this awful crime were never brought to light. Whatever the true facts of the case, the violence was highly untypical of child-stripping by women.

Women were uniquely placed to be child-strippers because they could use expectation about femininity to illicit trust from children. Women were also much more easily able to dispose of the proceeds of child-stripping than their male counterparts. Pawnbrokers or private buyers saw nothing suspicious of a mother who sold the shawls, boots or caps of a child. A man with a bundle of children's clothing would have more difficulty in explaining himself. Of course, some of the youngest child-strippers were initially little more than neighbourhood bullies taking small items and petty cash from their victims in order to buy sweets or pay for amusements. However, even those not much older than the children they robbed could be acting on behalf of family members or older offenders. Most child-strippers acted in full knowledge of the serious crime they committed and carefully honed their skills for this specialist offence.

Child-stripping was just one of several property offences that allowed female offenders to manipulate ideas about gender for their own gain.

Hocus pocus

The crime of 'hocussing' was known by several different names around the country and was the act of administering to a victim a substance that would produce a sleepy or stupefying quality, or otherwise render them insensible. The interesting name of the offence derives literally from the term 'hocus pocus' and carries with it all the connotations of trickery, hoodwinking and sleight of hand associated with magicians. Hocussing was a tactic used most often by thieves and occasionally in cases of sexual assault. The use of chloroform or laudanum mixed into gin by offenders gives this offence an undeniably Victorian feel but at the same time to be hocussed (or as we might refer to it, to have a drink 'spiked') is also a familiar peril in our own time. The practice of drugging victims for robbery, rape or kidnap has doubtlessly been used for centuries. What rendered hocussing so prevalent in the nineteenth century was the ease with which powerful drugs like morphine and laudanum might be acquired. Chemists sold cheap mixtures and tonics containing these substances over the counter; with few questions asked, powerful drugs could be acquired by anyone with enough money to buy them.

Hocussing was an offence popular with and used against both men and women. There was no strict gender divide for this crime. The appeal of the offence is easy to understand: a stupefied victim did not put up any resistance and could not raise the alarm. Hocussing was a particularly useful method for women because it allowed them greater opportunity to single-handedly perpetrate thefts against men without the need for physical force. Whilst some female offenders had the physical build to take on almost any male victim with force, others found it difficult to commit successful robberies against men who were often larger and stronger than themselves. Stupefying drugs and elixirs could overcome this issue. Men were rewarding targets for female thieves, whether they had watches and jewellery on their person or a week's pay packet stowed in their pocket.

It was not only the ability to overcome physical disadvantage that made hocussing appeal to female offenders. An unconscious or insensible victim gave an offender the opportunity to much more thoroughly search and obtain valuables and perhaps most importantly, to make a clean getaway. Women could commit a hocus in the safety of their own lodgings, in an alley after meeting a victim in a pub or coffee house, or even on a train. Anywhere women could gain access to victims for long enough to enjoy a drink with them, a successful hocus could be pulled off. By the time the victim came to, noticed their belongings were missing and raised the alarm, offenders could be away. Hocussing was perpetrated throughout the country (although like many property crimes had less success in small and rural locations where victims and offenders might know each other and live in close proximity). London, however, a large city with ample transport links, cabmen, pubs and anonymous lodging houses, was a particular haven for those that hocussed.

Margaret Navin met her victim James Maddington in December 1864 in a Stepney pub. The bar was crowded and when Maddington called for ale Margaret kindly said she would fetch it for him to save him the bother. When she returned with the ale Maddington treated her to a glass by way of thanks. As one thing led to another the two spent the evening drinking together. When the pub closed Margaret made it clear that she wished Maddington to come home with her for the evening. He gladly accepted and followed her home, where a number of other people joined them later. Maddington was plied with alcohol and as a final nightcap, Margaret served him a glass of gin. The drink contained a strong drug and it rendered Maddington insensible within minutes. When James Maddington came to sometime later, he found himself very ill and laying in a yard in an unfamiliar part of Stepney. Almost immediately, he noticed that his watch – worth £4 – was missing. Maddington went immediately to the police. Margaret was picked up by officers within forty-eight hours. When taken into custody Margaret was found to have twenty pawn tickets on her person. Each of the pawned items were watches and rings that had in all likelihood come from other victims treated just like Maddington. One police officer labelled Margaret 'a watch thief and the worst woman in the district'. Had Margaret carried out a successful robbery and received a few pounds for Maddington's watch she would have had ample cash with which to live well for a few weeks and to purchase her next stock of drugs.

Some of the most skilled hocussers used drugs that dissolved tastelessly in alcohol. Others with less experience could end up using a more abrasive concoction that burned the mouth when ingested. Foul-tasting or abrasive substances might tip off a potential victim before they were fully incapacitated, so in the vast majority of cases, hocussing was combined with alcohol. Drunk victims were less likely to realise they were being slipped a doctored drink than someone in possession of their full faculties. It was easiest for female offenders to pick up victims in a social setting such as a pub when inhibitions and awareness were already slightly lowered. When women picked their victims well, the suggestion of a night's company after last orders was seldom declined. Hocussing did not always arise from social situations though. Nor did it have to begin with something so cordial as a glass of gin. In extreme cases little more than a handkerchief and chloroform were needed to pull off the crime.

Frederick Jewett had been walking home late one night along the Whitechapel Road when he felt a woman tug at his left side. At the same time he felt a rag pressed over his mouth and nose. He fell unconscious almost immediately. When he awoke the next morning, he testified to finding himself on 'a very dirty bed in a wretched apartment in a complete state of nudity'. As he staggered about trying to make sense of his surroundings he found his trousers, which had been left over a chair. They were 'encrusted with mud up to the knees, as if he had been dragged forcibly along the road'. His watch, rings, money, coat, hat, boots and shawl were all missing.

Jewett had been locked inside a first-floor back room of a low lodging house in Spitalfields. After some shouting, he managed to attract attention from neighbours and with the help of several people was conveyed to the police so he could relay his ordeal to the authorities. Two women, Margaret Higgins and Elizabeth Smith, were found to have occupied that room but had since absconded. The pair were eventually tracked down. In preparing for the offence they had been less than discreet, speaking of their plans it seems to almost anyone that would listen. When Margaret was found she attempted to shift the blame onto Elizabeth, claiming that 'Fat Bet brought him to my room and after robbing him of his things she stuck to the regulars and never gave me anything.' Margaret told the police where they might find Elizabeth and added that she hoped the woman would be transported for the crime. When Elizabeth Smith was found she made exactly the same accusations towards Margaret Higgins. Evidence given by witnesses who had seen the two together, and the unlikelihood of either one of the women being able to drag an insensible Jewett to Spitalfields and up a flight of stairs alone, saw them both charged for the offence. It transpired that Margaret had obtained the chloroform from one of her associates who had stolen it from the London Hospital after undergoing an operation there. Both women were convicted.

The drugging of victims was not a precise art. Often the substances used were not tested for their strength or safety and those administering them had little care for dosage. From a hocusser's point of view it was far better to give too much sedative and have an easier time of robbery than to give too little and risk a victim coming round earlier than expected. Hocussers were liable to use anything in any quantity that would render a victim unconscious. It was uncommon but not unknown for victims to die from the effects of the substances administered to them.

Fredrick Lewis ran a brothel in Waterloo that a newspaper reported to be 'the residence of women of the worst character, and an intolerable nuisance to the respectable inhabitants of the locality'. Lewis was found dead in his kitchen having been drugged to death by his own lodgers with whom he had been up drinking the night before. By the time Lewis's wife found him on the kitchen floor the next day five women had fled from the house not to be seen again. Likewise, Thomas Robinson of Nottingham was hocussed by a prostitute named Hannah Hurd. Robinson had visited the brothel that Hannah worked in and she had laced his gin with three pence worth of laudanum so that she might pick his pocket. Robinson's unconscious body was left out in a yard later that day and he never regained full consciousness. He began frothing at the nose and mouth and died the following day. Hannah was transported for life.

Most cases of hocussing by women involved male victims, who were more likely to be found travelling alone or in pubs unaccompanied. Commonly held ideas about the strength of men and the weakness of women also saw men likely to be flattered rather than cautious of female attention and unlikely to be wary of finding themselves alone with a woman. After all, men were not only supposed to be physically stronger than women, but more intelligent, wise and cunning too. It was unusual for a Victorian man to feel threatened by a lone woman who wanted to share a drink with him. Exploiting these ideas allowed women to gain close and intimate access to male victims as they enticed them back to private lodgings with promises of drink and other entertainments. However, occasionally women too had cause to fear the female hocusser. Much as in cases of child-stripping, female hocussers exploited widely held stereotypes of women's maternal instinct and innate kindness to gain the trust of female victims.

Jane Mills was the 19-year-old daughter of a retired soldier and had come to the capital to look for a situation as a domestic servant. Near

London Bridge she was accosted by a middle-aged woman. The woman, after hearing Jane's story, advised her that it would be far more sensible to stay the night in London and make an early start of the search for work the next morning rather than returning home that evening. The woman offered her own home to serve as accommodation. Naïvely, Jane accepted the offer and proceeded with the woman towards the East End. On the way, the older women suggested that they take a drink in a pub as they passed. Inside Jane was given two glasses of gin and 'from that time until seven o'clock the following morning she was perfectly unconscious.' Jane woke up, completely naked, in a filthy communal toilet. She was discovered by a policeman and taken to the station house to recover. Jane could remember nothing after being in the pub. The culprit responsible for her hocussing was never found.

How common hocussing was compared to other forms of theft from the person is hard to know. Cases of stealing from a drugged victim came to court less often than other kinds of theft from the person but this does not necessarily mean that the number of acts were as minimal as the number of prosecutions. As shown by the case of poor Jane Mills, hocussing allowed for an easy escape. If offenders were clever enough not to use their own lodgings or work in their own neighbourhood there was very little chance of tracing them hours or days after the event. Confusion and memory loss after a drugging may have prevented victims seeking help at all. Many hocussers will have escaped the notice of history that way. The second reason we know relatively little about the women who hocussed and how they did it is the reluctance of victims to come forward. Married men who had gone home with a strange woman from the pub often chose to 'lose' a watch or a few shillings rather than explain their circumstances to friends and family. Likewise, embarrassed students, doctors and clerks who were hocussed while visiting bad neighbourhoods or brothels chose not to come forward and have their details known in news reports or in court. By exploiting social ideas about gender and respectability, hocussing provided a way for women to steal with a reduced likelihood of prosecution.

Fraud, forgery and confidence

Women's manipulation of ideas about female passivity and innocence did not stop with robbing single men and small children. The uncanny ability of some female offenders to gain the confidence of their victims could stretch to much larger and longer-term thefts. Women's almost complete exclusion from the financial world, from banking and business, in the Victorian period meant that whilst women were not considered particularly financially able they were also unlikely to be suspected of purposely conducting fraudulent transactions.

Fraud, forgery and confidence tricks made up a small minority of female property offences in this period because of the difficulty women could face in interacting in the financial world. Most ordinary women lacked the social status to deal in large financial transactions. Although it was not completely unknown for women to pull off high value confidence tricks, insurance frauds or embezzlements most crimes of fraud and forgery took place at a much lower level. Primarily this was because most working-class women (who made up the vast majority of female offenders) lacked the experience and materials to pull off an elaborate and costly deception. Quite simply, a poor woman with limited means for presenting herself would find practical difficulty in interacting in the elite financial world with bankers, lawyers and businessmen. The types of fraud that the average female offender was able to perpetrate without good name, correct presentation and the right contacts included a plethora of small tricks and thefts such as forging payment for household items, or servant women purportedly acting on their employer's behalf when acquiring jewellery, money or goods, and even blackmail.

Con artists from the Continent

Eliza Welzenstein and her husband Edward were both born in Austria in the early 1830s. There they had lived a comfortable life. Edward was a military officer and Eliza was the daughter of a military family. Edward was dismissed from the military either for fighting a duel or being too free with his political opinions. Some suggested both. The Welzensteins had then made their way around the world through Germany, Belgium, England,

and even America, living any way they could. The Welzensteins settled in London first and there lived off the proceeds of regular frauds by leaving in their wake 'frequent changes of residence, debts, difficulties, pawnings, assumptions of names and titles'.

In 1860, Eliza, with Edward and two other accomplices – a man named Freak and a woman known simply as 'Madam Jordan' – appeared at the Old Bailey. The four had been charged with attempting to 'cheat and defraud' a respectable tailor. The tailor, a man by the name of Mr Stohwasser, was a fellow Austrian and it was said that he took a great interest in the welfare of his countrymen. Stohwasser was introduced to the Welzensteins, Freak and Jordan by a member of the German Benevolent Society. Touched by the tale of hardship they told, for a long period of time Stohwasser 'lavished money upon them' and provided a fully furnished house for the group to live in as well as ensuring medical assistance came to Eliza Welzenstein when she fell ill. Not only did Stohwasser take care of all of the group's living expenses, he also provided money to Freak so that he might travel abroad to recover some of the property and fortune he claimed was lost. Eliza Welzenstein, Freak and Jordan proceeded to squander the money and pawn some of the furniture provided by their host. Further to this, Eliza endeavoured to seduce Stohwasser and have Freak and her husband Edward discover them together so that they might extort money from him to avoid a scandal. When the fraud was discovered, Edward Welzenstein and Freak both received two years' imprisonment, and Eliza and Jordan were given six months' hard labour.

In 1862, Edward was still in prison, and Eliza had arranged to make a living as a lady's maid in the service of a Captain Williams Frazer. There, Eliza was prosecuted for stealing a quantity of 'wines, spirits and linen' from her employer. She attempted to throw blame for the offence onto Captain Frazer's butler. Eliza was, however, no stranger to the prosecutor and was quickly found guilty. The prosecutor went to great lengths after the verdict was read – but before a sentence was passed – to recount the details of Eliza's 1860 conviction. For the current offence of stealing from Captain Frazer, Welzenstein was given four years' penal servitude. The prosecution had succeeded in ensuring that Eliza's sentence reflected not only the offence she had carried out against Captain Frazer but also the kind of poor moral character she was perceived to have.

Eliza remained in London after her release from prison in 1866. The potential anonymity provided by the sprawling metropolis was a convenient cover for former convicts looking to obtain employment or carry out further offences without detection. It was almost four years until Eliza was again apprehended and returned to court in 1870. Eliza had once more obtained a position with a prestigious employer, this time a barrister in Grosvenor Square, from whom she had been able to steal over £100 worth of buttons, lace and other accessories. Eliza also faced a second charge for stealing handkerchiefs and other small items from a previous employer in Hyde Park. Then a third charge was presented against Eliza. A Mrs Loftie of Portman Square identified forks found in Eliza's possession when she was arrested, and stated that Eliza must have taken them when working for her as a servant. Eliza continued to find positions as a domestic servant, even after dismissal for theft or criminal conviction, by means of forged character references. When committed for trial for the multiple thefts, Eliza was also told that she would face another charge for her use of fraudulent references. Eliza was sentenced to seven years' penal servitude. She was released in 1875 but in the following years her health declined and she died in Hackney in 1879.

Eliza Welzenstein was not the only European woman to arrive in England's capital with a mind to make easy profit from the ample opportunities for fraud. At the same time Eliza's name was receiving interest by the English press, a French woman and her husband were gaining notoriety as international art thieves.

Amelie Decuypere, or Amelia, as she was also known, had been convicted alongside her husband Paul in 1859 for the theft of several articles worth upwards of £35 from the house of a man named Raymond Collins. According to the court, this had been the latest in a long line of similar offences. Whilst they were on trial for this offence alone, the prosecutor suggested 'at least a dozen could have been brought forward by the police'. Amelie and Paul had a well-practised scheme; they would take well-furnished lodgings, and make off with the contents of the house at the first available opportunity. Like other offenders, they had many other names under which they worked, but each was more distinctive than the last. The couple worked as Amelie and Paul Thuillier, and a marriage licence signed by the mayor of Paris in 1849 revealed that in fact they might be Antoine Thuillier and Louise Claudine Margaret.

These two Parisians were not just ordinary house thieves or servants with light fingers. An inspector of the Metropolitan Police provided evidence that a year previously they had stolen, from the museum of Amsterdam, a painting of a religious scene, worth £2,000 (about £90,000 today). They were apprehended in London but due to no treaty of extradition existing between England and the Netherlands, there was no choice but to release them without charge. Evidence was also found that in Paris a trial of both Amelie and Paul had been held, despite their absence, and they had been convicted of 'swindling' and 'fraudulent bankruptcy' and sentenced to ten and twenty years' hard labour respectively.

A document sent from the French government to England while the Decuyperes served their sentences indicated that once released, they were to be deported to France so that their standing sentences of imprisonment could be served. A special request was even made that Paul not be listed for transportation to Western Australia so that the French legal system could extract its own justice. Amelie Decuypere was paroled from Fulham Prison in 1864, having served five years of a six-year sentence. Her licence was not revoked, and no note was made of her having been returned to prison. There is no trace of Amelie or her husband after her release from prison and, we must suppose, her extradition back to France went ahead.

In a small number of cases where circumstances allowed, the frauds women committed could be extensive and notorious, reaching into the highest echelons of society. Female offenders that had the wherewithal to present themselves as women of means, or who had the contacts to interact with the more elite sections of society, could carry out frauds and forgeries worth thousands of pounds. Women at the higher end of financial crime might forge bills of sale for property they did not own, or pay for expensive items of jewellery with faulty bank notes or cheques. A relatively common deception was to sign over a fraudulent cheque to an unsuspecting businessman or legal professional in way of part payment for goods or services and at the same time asking for a small portion of the cheque's value in cash. A few exceptional women were able to perpetrate frauds based on confidence and the loyalty of their customers for decades in plain sight of the Victorian establishment.

Beautiful for ever

Sarah Rachel Leverson was born into a Jewish family in America in the 1820s. In later life as a widow, she and her children arrived in England. She wasted little time in setting up a lucrative cosmetics business in London's fashionable and wealthy Bond Street. The salon began trading in 1863 and operated under the name 'Beautiful For Ever'. Madame Rachel, as she became known, was such an important figure in the world of women's cosmetics that powders on sale almost a century later still bore her name. However, she was not only a beautician to the rich and influential, but also the perpetrator of a series of frauds against her high society customers.

By cunning advertising proclaiming that she supplied perfumes and toiletries to the Royal Family, Madame Rachel's business soon became the talk of London and wealthy customers flocked through her doors. Goods and treatments offered in Madame Rachel's store could cost many hundreds of pounds. For a few years, this lucrative trade earned her an enviable reputation and her business thrived. In 1865, Frederick Bevor attempted to extort money from Madame Rachel by threatening to publish a libel about her that would damage her pristine reputation and thus her business. Wise already to the ways of fraud, Madame Rachel refused to give him any money and took him to court, where he was found guilty of extortion and sentenced to three months in prison.

It was less than three years later that Madame Rachel herself would stand in the very same dock, charged with fraud and false pretences. In 1868, she went on trial at the Old Bailey for obtaining large sums of money and goods from Mary Tucker Borrodaile. It was a conspiracy worth an estimated £3,000. In the context of the time, this was a huge amount of money, which is equivalent today to more than £100,000.

Mary Tucker Borrodaile was the widow of an army colonel who had first made Madame Rachel's acquaintance after returning from India, where her husband had been stationed. She met Madame Rachel in 1864. Knowing her as the 'perfumer' to Queen Victoria, Mary attended Madame Rachel's shop in Bond Street. Here she purchased 'powders and two or three boxes of soaps' for her beauty regime. Mary became a repeat customer of Madame Rachel's, visiting her twice for supplies in 1865. The following year, Mary visited again in hopes of finding a solution for her skin problems and in a conversation with Madame Rachel was asked how much money she had to spend. The reply inferred that money would be little object. When she called again two days later, Madame Rachel had some surprising news for her. Mary recounted, 'She told me a gentleman loved me; Lord Ranelagh. I was very much surprised.' A meeting was arranged between Lord Ranelagh and Mary for a few days later.

In the coming weeks Mary and the mysterious Lord Ranelagh were often thrown together by Madame Rachel, and Mary was told by Madame Rachel that Ranelagh wished to marry her. Madame Rachel convinced Mary of the happiness and fortune to be found in such a match. Then one day the following month, Madame Rachel, according to Mary, 'said it was necessary that I should be made beautiful for ever, before I married Lord Ranelagh; for if not, it would only be money thrown away, and I should be sent to the country where I should never be seen.' Madame Rachel also suggested that for the princely sum of £1,000 Mary's beautification and happiness could be achieved. The bulk of the sum was dutifully retrieved from a bank and paid to Madame Rachel. Mary then began receiving a number of forged love letters. They were signed in different names but all, according to Madame Rachel, came from Lord Ranelagh. An exchange of letters continued for some time and over the course of her correspondence with Lord Ranelagh, Mary was induced to pay a further £1,400 for Madame Rachel's services to make her 'beautiful for ever'.

By February of 1867, Mary had not been rendered any more beautiful than before her treatments (mainly soap washes and herb–infused baths) had begun. The letters from Ranelagh had disappeared and Mary's communication with Madame Rachel had stopped. It took more than a year for a disappointed and embarrassed Mary Tucker Borrodaile to get her day in court against Madame Rachel. The case was examined in minute and humiliating detail. The letters had all been forgeries, there had never been an offer of marriage, and the money was gone. Madame Rachel declined to give a statement in defence. After five hours, the jury were dismissed, unable to reach a verdict.

A month later, a new trial began. This time it was for the charge of obtaining goods and money to the value of just £600 by false pretences, and only for conspiring to defraud Mary of £3,000. The evidence of the letters and testimony of the hundreds of baths Mary had taken at Madame Rachel's instructions were all heard again. Madame Rachel was found guilty and sentenced to five years' imprisonment. The following year, even as she served time in prison, further complainants came forward claiming to have been defrauded by Madame Rachel. It became clear that she had obtained money not just from Mary, but many thousands of pounds from the wealthy and well connected.

Madame Rachel's connections with the rich and elite of high society ensured that the case made national news. The fraud even became the subject of a satirical play. Madame Rachel's case was so notorious it continued to be mentioned in national newspapers well into the twentieth century. Such a fantastical deception rendered her a noted trickster and surely should have put an end to future frauds. Even if imprisonment was not enough to discourage Madame Rachel from further frauds, recognition should have made it virtually impossible to perpetrate a future crime of the same nature without a change in name or location.

However, after her release from prison Madame Rachel rented new premises in Grosvenor Square and began to trade again. She even placed a sign above her shop that once more proclaimed her an 'Arabian Perfumer to the Queen'. In 1876, Cecilia Maria Pearse, a visitor from Rome, was calling on a doctor in Duke Street, Grosvenor Square, when she noticed Madame Rachel's shop. She went in and purchased tooth powder and violet powder. On returning to the shop another time Cecilia purchased a few bottles of face wash costing several pounds.

When Cecilia returned the following year, she found Madame Rachel again at new premises in Great Portland Street. Madame Rachel suggested it would be best for Cecilia not to mention their acquaintance to her husband given that she had been 'wrongfully' convicted some years previously, and even though she had 'cleared her name before the public' she did not want to attract undue attention to herself. Cecilia continued to buy products for her skin from Madame Rachel, who told her how youthful they would keep her. Madame Rachel claimed it had done the very same for her, telling Cecilia she was, in fact, eighty-five (she was about fifty-eight at this time). In the first year of their connection, Cecilia had spent about £20 on remedies for her poor complexion with Madame Rachel.

In December 1877, Cecilia developed a rash on her face. Sensing an opportunity, Madam Rachel told her that the condition of her skin was grave and that if she did not complete her treatments at the shop, her complexion would be ruined for life. Madame Rachel stated that her usual fee for this course of treatments was £1,000 but that as she and Cecilia were friends, the price could be lowered to £500. Cecilia at first declined, to which Madame Rachel is said to have stated, 'Very well, you will be sorry in later life: and I warn you, you are in such a state that if you put even cold cream or water on your face you will be disfigured for life.' On these words, the two women parted.

A distressed Cecilia Pearse returned to Madame Rachel sometime later. Madame Rachel made a final offer to charge just £200 to finish treatment on her skin. The same treatment, she said, had cost the aristocratic Lady Dudley £2,000. Thinking herself lucky to receive the offer of such a discount, Cecilia agreed. To pay part of the debt, Cecilia eventually ended up giving Madame Rachel her jewellery. As this was not enough to cover the entire cost, slowly but surely, Madame Rachel made further demands for money. Cecilia became increasingly distressed at her inability to meet the demands and eventually turned to her husband. Mr Pearse engaged a solicitor and the case was brought to court.

Madame Rachel was found guilty and sentenced to another five years of penal servitude. A pharmacist also testified that whilst Madame Rachel's creams and treatments were largely harmless and not responsible for causing Cecilia's skin complaint, they were mostly ineffectual at producing any of the results Madame Rachel had promised. Madame Rachel was sent back to prison, where she died two years later in October 1880.

Women like Eliza Welzenstein, Amelie Decuypere and Sarah Rachel Leverson often arrived in England after notable careers of crime in their country of origin and elsewhere. The absence of quick or efficient communication between authorities across nations, unchecked travel and very few photographs of offenders that could be widely circulated meant that moving country was the most efficient way for those intending to live by fraud and forgery. London was a melting pot of men and women from across Europe and the British Empire. This rendered offenders like Eliza, Amelie and Sarah no more noticeable than the thousands of other inhabitants – until they chose to be so. What's more, with social prejudice and police preoccupation largely looking for crime amongst England's native poor, the foreign criminal with a good enough backstory might go undetected for years.

These cases of fraud, of course, are an extreme example of the kinds of deception that women were able to commit. Yet they do offer a pertinent reminder that female offenders were only too willing to exploit ideas of female financial ineptitude and middle-class respectability to make money. The majority of female fraudsters targeted less 'important' victims, who were less likely to have the time and means to bring an effective prosecution, and smaller value frauds that presented less risk. The lack of prosecutions of women for this kind of offence may be due, just as in the case of hocussing, to the reluctance of male victims of respectable standing to expose themselves to a trial and the embarrassment of having been conned by a member of the supposedly weaker, gentler and less intelligent sex.

Ungrateful girls

Theft by a servant was among the most risky of property crimes for women. There was a virtual certainty that discovery of the crime would lead to the loss of employment because it happened in the workplace and was an offence against employers. The culprits of thefts from private homes were also easy to identify. When household items and valuables began to go missing just as a new member of staff arrived or left employment, the implications were clear. Thus, the likelihood of the crime being discovered and the culprit being identified was higher than with other kinds of theft.

The increased risks associated with stealing from employers did not put off as many offenders as we might assume. Incidents of thefts by servants remained high throughout the nineteenth century and this offence seems to have been particularly appealing to women. The spectre of the light-fingered housemaid caused significant concern to employers who were already wary of giving the lower classes access to the most intimate areas of their homes and lives. Character references were necessary for most potential employers looking to take on new staff but this was far from a foolproof system. Some women were able to gain employment and steal from multiple households before discovery, and even after imprisonment. After a conviction it was unlikely (although by no means impossible) that a woman would be able to work as domestic servant again.

I wish I could have resisted temptation

Mary Ann Reed was born into a family of agricultural workers in Suffolk. She was one of six siblings in an ordinary rural community. As the Reed children grew up, the boys took on farm work with their father and the girls were forced to look for employment outside the small village of Kirton.

Like other young women looking to make their way in the world, Mary Ann headed to London in her late teens with the intention of getting a job as a domestic servant. By the age of eighteen Mary had managed to establish herself as a servant in a respectable lodging house in Marylebone under the employment of a Mrs Turner. However, the reality of the poor pay and long hours involved in domestic work soon saw the job lose its appeal. A house that provided an ever-changing stream of visitors and residents put in Mary Ann's way the opportunity of rich pickings to be pilfered. Mary Ann soon succumbed to temptation and began to store various items of stolen property in a box in her room. The mistress of the house quickly discovered the items and Mary Ann begged for forgiveness. Surprisingly, Mrs Turner took pity on Mary Ann and granted her a second chance on the condition that all the items be restored to their owners. A tearful Mary Ann agreed, but as Mrs Turner went to ask forgiveness from her lodgers, Mary Ann seized the opportunity to re-steal some of the items that were to be returned. On discovery, Mary Ann was immediately turned out of the house, but luckily for her, no charges were brought.

Not only was Mary Ann lucky enough to avoid prosecution for this first offence, she also somehow managed to gain another situation as a servant in the very same street. She worked for another eighteen months before finding herself in trouble again. In 1870, along with another employee, Ellen Vincent, a girl of just sixteen, Mary Ann stole a bank bill for the sum of £50 out of her master's post. Mary Ann and Ellen had headed straight to a draper's shop and obtained material for new dresses. They attempted to pay with the stolen bill and asked for the remaining value – more than £40 – in change. When the deception was discovered they were both arrested. Mary Ann was recognised as the mastermind of the scheme and given twelve months in prison. Ellen, who it was clear to see had been led astray by Mary, was given four months.

By 1871, Mary Ann had returned for a third time to working as a servant. Almost unbelievably she had managed to gain another position as a maid just two streets away from the homes of the last two employers she had stolen from. Mary Ann worked in this new house for about a year – just enough time to make the acquaintance of a new partner in crime. This time her accomplice was 19-year-old Harriet Hall. Mary Ann began stealing small items from the house and passing them on in exchange for cash. The property had been missed but her employer lacked the proof to make an accusation. Mary Ann was only found out when she stole a cheque worth £10 from a lady visiting the house. Mary Ann got Harriet to forge the signature required for endorsement of the cheque and then went to cash it in at the butcher's. Unused to being paid for meat with such a large sum of money, the butcher was suspicious and raised the alarm. Mary Ann was apprehended and tried to deflect the blame on to Harriet. When this tactic was unsuccessful she attempted and failed to bribe the officer for her freedom. Mary's previous criminal record exposed the case for what it was. The court showed no mercy on the third offence of a dishonest servant and Mary was sentenced to seven years' imprisonment. Again, her accomplice was believed to have been led astray and only received four months.

Mary Ann served five years in prison before being sent to the Russell House Refuge for rehabilitation for the remainder of her sentence. Her conduct in the refuge was so good that the superintendent felt moved to acquire Mary Ann a new domestic service position for when she was released. A job was found for Mary Ann with a Mrs Briggs in Hampstead and she began work there in 1877. Within a year, Mary Ann was found to have stolen a £10 note, a £5 note, £19 in sovereigns and diamond pins. In total, the value of the theft was about £74 – the biggest haul that Mary Ann had ever attempted. Mary Ann had been storing the stolen items in the house and when suspicion fell upon her she sent a forged letter from Victoria Station claiming the goods had been found on a platform there and were ready to be returned. Mrs Briggs was not fooled and after searching Mary Ann's room found some of the stolen property. Mary Ann had attempted to burn the rest in a fire. After her arrest Mary tried to cast the blame onto another woman whom she had met in the Russell House Refuge, but this too was proved to be false. When the full details of the crime were discovered Mary Ann's only defence was, 'I wish I could have resisted temptation.' Mary Ann was sentenced to ten years in prison. (See plate 8.)

When she was released in the late 1880s, Mary Ann returned to live with family in Suffolk, far away from service and the temptation of strangers' belongings. Marry Ann Reed's career as a thieving servant was remarkable for its longevity and also for the persistence she showed in stealing from her employers. What is more surprising is the fact that, despite her criminal record, she was able to obtain three domestic service jobs in close succession within the same neighbourhood, and even a fourth still within London, after spending five years in prison.

In many ways, thefts by servants like Mary Ann Reed are some of the hardest to understand. Child-strippers and those carrying out hocusses might have turned to crime as a result of unemployment or financial crisis that affected their ability to pay for accommodation or food, but domestic servants not only received a reliable wage but many received bed and board also. Domestic service was amongst the most securely paid employment for working-class women available in the Victorian period. Whilst it was seldom enjoyable or well paid, it did offer women a certain amount of security. What the cases of thieving servants show us is that often offences were the result of little more than opportunism. They could be impulsive crimes, where temptation proved too much.

Thieving servants didn't always have to be full time, live-in, or permanent members of staff. Sarah Street, a 28-year-old charwoman (a woman who cleaned the homes of others on a casual basis for a very small fee), worked for her employer Mr Greenwood just one day a week but managed to steal velvet, a shawl, dozens of knives and other articles over the course of several visits. Those with the greatest access to valuables and the easiest opportunities to steal did however tend to be those servants who resided in their employers' homes and spent their days carrying out unsupervised work around the house.

Servants who were convicted of stealing from their employers were comparatively young women when compared to others who committed different kinds of property crime. Such thefts might act as a gateway to more serious or prolonged episodes of property crime. There were, of course, women who had served honestly for many years, who were eventually induced by want or need to steal and lost their positions. However, overwhelmingly, theft by servants saw women from the ages of fifteen to twenty-two in the dock. These young women were often those in their first appointments as servants. In many cases, the women had become frustrated with their long hours of work, low pay or demanding nature of their employers, and had stolen items to redress these perceived injustices.

Henry Mayhew's investigation of the thieving servant revealed:

> Many felonies are committed by domestic female servants who have been only a month or six months in service. Some of them steal tea, sugar and other provisions, which are frequently given to acquaintances or relatives out of doors. Others occasionally abstract linen and articles of wearing-apparel, or plunder the wardrobe of gold bracelets, rings, pearl necklace, watch, chain or other jewellery, or of muslin and silk dresses and mantles, which they either keep in their trunk or otherwise dispose of.

Some servants stole under the encouragement of others. Sarah Ann Bradley, an 18-year-old servant from Dudley, had been induced by her older sister Elizabeth to steal a range of items from her employer including hairbrushes, hairnets, perfume and combs. Sarah Ann would pass the pilfered items to Elizabeth, who would then sell or pawn them. A trail of witnesses led the police back to Sarah, who, in her own words, explained, 'I did take them; my sister asked me to get them for her and she would give me the money to pay for them.' Elizabeth claimed she did not know the articles were stolen and that they were given to her at different times over a period of two months by Sarah, who had said that young men in her employer's shop gave them to her as gifts. It is impossible to say for sure where the truth lies for this offence, but it was likely a joint enterprise between the sisters.

Other servants, for the sake of ease and discretion, acted alone. In Bristol in 1858, 26-year-old Harriet Pocock was convicted of stealing a needle book, a silver knife, napkins, a flannel petticoat, a bogwood brooch, a stone ring, a collar and other items totalling in value £1 17s. 6d., all belonging to her master, Samuel Prounce. With the exception of the jewellery, no one of these items was particularly valuable; the value was in the quantity of her theft. It is more than likely that instead of one concentrated episode of theft, Harriet had been slowly accumulating her employer's belongings over a period of time by taking individual items when the opportunity presented itself. It often took some time to detect the activities of servants who stole in this way; only when the hoard of their illicitly acquired goods was discovered, or they were caught in the act of stealing them, did their multiple thefts come to light. On her apprehension, Harriet was given four years of penal servitude for her offence, which was not her first. The previous year, Harriet had been on trial for committing theft from her master in Bristol. Over the course of her employment, she had managed to steal from him 8 yards of ribbon, two handkerchiefs, a chemise, a veil and a needle case. For the first of her thefts, Harriet only spent three months in prison.

One of the biggest risks to servants was losing their reputation for good character, as judged by their employers for poor work or dishonesty. A character reference given by employers would allow servants to seek new positions. However, the importance of a reference from a previous employer seems to have been somewhat overstated. As cases like Harriet Pocock's and Mary Ann Reed's illustrate, even lengthy terms of imprisonment would not automatically exclude a woman from finding future employment as a domestic servant. There was also the distinct possibility that those women willing to steal from their employers were also willing to forge character references or lie at interviews for future jobs.

There were other servants who stole for more pressing reasons. Jemima Ashton, a servant from Birmingham, appeared in court in 1860 with a baby in her arms. She had been apprehended for stealing silver-plated tableware from her previous employer. Jemima was in her thirties and was already well known to the court. There is little more recorded about Jemima's case and the six months she served in prison on this occasion. We can perhaps infer from the few details we do have that Jemima stole upon realising that she was unlikely to keep her position and income once her baby was born. It was not unknown for women about to leave or lose their employment to take the opportunity to secure funds while they still could. Four years later, Jemima was again in court for a very similar offence and received a sentence of another four years' imprisonment.

Average wages for a general domestic servant or 'maid of all work' in a small household might be from five to ten shillings a week. For this a female servant might be expected to work a six and a half-day week, labouring from before the sun rose until late each night. The work could involve physically hard tasks such as scrubbing, sweeping, carpet beating and washing. It is not difficult to appreciate that those undertaking punishing work for low pay in a house full of valuable items might be tempted to steal. The value of a few small items such as a brooch, silver knife or handkerchief could amount to more than a week's or month's wage.

A note on arson

Stealing was by no means the worst property crime that a servant might carry out against her employer; stolen goods might at least be recovered. Disgruntled female servants causing damage to property was a more serious matter. The most extreme cases of damage to property occurred when servants set fire to their mistress's or master's furniture, or even their entire house, in an act of revenge for poor treatment or dismissal. Arson occupies an odd hinterland between violence and property crime. The act of setting fire to a dwelling or property is undeniably a violent one; the aim is not profit but destruction, to say nothing of the life-threatening danger a fire can cause. Yet in the Victorian courts, it was the cost of the damage, as well as the fact that the sanctity of private property had been violated, that seemed to most outrage judges and juries. Female arsonists commonly received sentences of five to ten years' imprisonment for their acts.

Servants living in rural locations seem to have been the most prone to setting fire to stacks of produce belonging to their masters. For instance, 18-year-old Ellen Atkin (see plate 9) from Yorkshire set fire to a stack of her master's barley. Likewise, 16-year-old Edith Jennings from Gloucestershire set fire to her master's haystacks on two consecutive evenings. To all accounts her employers were kind to her and she gave no reason for her crime, initially attempting to push the blame onto a passing stranger. It seemed as if the arson, costing her employer several hundred pounds, was little more than the result of a workplace annoyance. Similarly, Selina Greening, a 17-year-old also from Gloucestershire, set fire to her employer's wheat for much the same reason.

Arson was a rare occurrence but when it did happen in rural locations, it tended to follow this exact pattern of produce burning. It was almost always a first-time offence. The young women who started such fires may have wanted to send a message or get one up on their employers but probably did not realise the full financial cost and subsequent repercussions of their actions. In more urban and suburban environments, it was houses and furniture that bore the brunt of arsonists' rage, with fires often spiralling out of control and damaging far more than was intended. Eighteen-year-old Sarah Ann Nash was brought up at the Old Bailey in 1870 charged with setting fire to a house with intent to injure. Sarah had been working for a Mr and Mrs Capes in Hammersmith but had been given her notice to leave the position. On her final day at work Sarah gathered up large amounts of her employers' furniture and other possessions in two downstairs rooms and set them on fire. Unbeknown to Sarah, both Mr and Mrs Capes were out of the house all day and only returned to their smouldering home late that evening. Sarah's fire was an act of revenge for being dismissed and an attempt to cover up the thefts she made from the house as she was leaving, but it spiraled out of control. She received five years in prison.

Servants probably made up the biggest group of female arsonists in this era, but the other significant use of arson by women was for the purposes of insurance fraud. Usually in conspiracy with husbands or partners, women would insure goods or property and then set a fire with the intention of making a false claim. Even during an age in which forensic investigation was in its infancy, insurance companies and investigators were wise to the scams of would-be claimants. Most of the women who were caught attempting to make false claims for accidental fire damage were found out when investigation revealed the place where the fire started and even the materials used to cause the blaze.

Moneymaking

In a world in which money was hard to come by even through legitimate means one of the simplest solutions available to women seeking to earn a living was literally to make money. Without many of the methods of detecting forgery and false currency that we have available today the production of counterfeit money was possible for anyone who could source the relatively common materials it required.

The forgery of bank notes, cheques and bank drafts could earn counterfeiters large amounts of money quickly, but successfully creating useable false notes and passing them off as genuine presented several difficulties and did not have good long-term prospects. There were only so many shops, banks and establishments that would cash high value notes and most would become suspicious about doing so for the same customer multiple times in quick succession. When a forgery was discovered, the culprit could be easily traced. Offenders would not be able to return to the same premises again or to approach others in the nearby vicinity for some time after a forged bank note was offered. Once stung by an expensive forgery, shopkeepers were likely to be on their guard with high value transactions. What is more, not many offenders would have the right appearance or credibility to make high value payments. Malnourished women in tattered dresses would raise suspicion if they tried to buy groceries with £50 notes or endorse cheques worth larger sums.

Counterfeit coins were a different matter altogether. Their face value – just pence and shillings each – was much smaller than the notes, cheques and bank drafts at the top of the counterfeiting ladder. It took more work to make a good profit from counterfeit coins. Yet the major advantage of smaller currency was that it might be placed into circulation with more ease. The number of locations at which bad coins could be tendered without causing suspicion was greater and the timeframe in which any group of offenders might carry out such offences was indefinite. With the right tools and network of accomplices, offenders could make a lifelong living from counterfeit coins.

The practice of coining in the Victorian period is one of the criminal activities we know most about. So prominent was the problem of false currency, especially in London, that there were special police divisions and detectives employed to protect the interests of the Royal Mint. Prosecutions for coining offences throughout the era were very common. The broad term of coining actually relates to two offences involving counterfeit currency. The first one in which women most commonly took the lead was in 'uttering' bad coins. Utterers used the counterfeit coins in shops and pubs to buy produce and to obtain change in good currency. The second offence, which was harder to detect and invariably involved more than one offender at a time, was in manufacturing or 'casting' counterfeit currency.

Uttering

As a form of property crime, uttering counterfeit coins, or 'smashing', was as simple as it could get for female offenders. Uttering did not require physical strength or agility. Women didn't have to be good at sleight of hand or constructing false identities. An utterer simply had to pay for goods with what appeared to be legitimate currency. The venues and values in which women uttered their false coins could vary but almost uniformly followed a pattern. Goods that cost significantly less than the face value of the forged coin would be purchased. The goods would be received along with change in legitimate currency. The utterer would leave and either keep the earnings, or pass the profit on to agents or those who made the coins, receiving a small amount back in payment. Women might take a share of each individual coin, or more likely be given a share of the profit from the total batch of bad coins made. Utterers would receive a number of counterfeit coins in one go and would attempt to offload them as efficiently as possible, so that they could earn a quick profit and avoid being found with false coins upon their person. Whilst coins could be passed almost anywhere, the most common location was in pubs.

In 1868, Susan Bailey was charged at the Old Bailey with uttering a bad shilling. She had been in a local pub with a friend and had used a fake shilling to buy a quarter of gin. This was a common tactic amongst coiners, who would buy readily consumable products like cheap food or drinks for just a few pennies. Each time they would pay with a bad coin and receive the change in good coins. If several different venues were used over the course of a day and the bad coins went undetected, a generous living could be accumulated in change and a day of free drinking could be had. Susan had been in a neighbouring establishment a day previously and had purchased a quart of gin with a counterfeit shilling. The landlady on that occasion had noticed and confronted her. This could often happen to coiners – especially those who dealt in poorly made and cheap replicas. In most cases, the offender would feign ignorance and apologise, producing the correct amount of money in good currency. Most of the time this was enough to allay suspicion.

Susan's mistake, like many of those coiners who found themselves caught out, was to target businesses in the same area repeatedly over a short period. When she bought her gin the following day at a new pub the barmaid recognised a bad shilling and it did not take long for talk to confirm her transactions in the neighbourhood the previous day. Susan received twelve months in prison. The previous year, Susan had been charged along with her partner Charles Philips and found to have a counterfeit coin in her possession. The charge of having the intention to utter could not be proved, so she had been freed with a verdict of not guilty.

Less than a year after her release from prison for the bad shilling, Susan was back at the Old Bailey again for uttering counterfeit coins in exactly the same circumstances. For passing a bad shilling to a barman for just two pence worth of gin, she was handed over to the police. As it was her third appearance in court she was sentenced to five years in prison. After her release, Susan did not pursue a career in passing counterfeit money. Years in prison had illustrated that she had neither the skill nor the anonymity to become a successful coiner. Susan did not renounce offending, though. In 1876, she had relocated to West Yorkshire, where she was sentenced to another five years' imprisonment for fraud. She had obtained 12 yards of fabric, boots and a number of umbrellas under false pretences in Wakefield. She offended again in 1881.

The formulaic nature of coining offences like Susan's seems to cross both time and location. In 1872, Caroline Johnson of Sheffield had gone to a local drinking place and ordered two pence worth of gin, paying for it with a counterfeit sixpence. Caroline protested that she had no knowledge of the money being bad but she was nevertheless sentenced to six months' imprisonment. Her subsequent criminal record indicates that this first offence was probably not accidental as she claimed, but one of many deliberate crimes by an established utterer. The next time Caroline was in court it was 1877, when she had been working as a servant in Sheffield, and she was sentenced to a year in prison for uttering a counterfeit coin. Two years later, Caroline was again in court, this time with her husband John, for passing more coins. In 1881, she received five years' imprisonment for uttering two bad sixpences to local tradesmen and then returning a few days later to one of the men to utter a bad shilling. (See plate 10.) Caroline only had four criminal convictions to her name, with years in between each of them in which we cannot know where she was or how she was making a living. It remains most likely that Caroline uttered many more bad coins during these years but was never caught. Often it was only chance or bad luck on the utterer's part, that saw forged coins recognised and seized. Women tended to be caught if they were too repetitive with the businesses they targeted, or too careless in how much money they attempted to pass at one time or with whom they tried to pass it. Attempts at uttering by women who were drunk often ended in apprehension as they had a tendency to argue with vendors over the legitimacy of their coins. There was an advanced risk of discovery for women who worked with poor forgeries.

Laura Reardon received five years of penal servitude in 1869 after pleading guilty at the Old Bailey to possessing counterfeit coins with intent to utter. No sooner had she been released from prison then she again began dealing in bad coins. Laura was arrested again, this time under the name of Martha English for uttering a fake half-crown. Laura had first attempted to buy a half loaf of bread from a baker in Peckham. Upon biting the coin with his teeth (a common way to test for coins made out of soft substandard metal) the baker declared it to be bad. Laura apologised, left the bread and took the bad coin away with her. Within half an hour of visiting the baker, Laura tried her luck at a butcher's shop only about 200 yards away. She attempted to buy some heart with the same bad crown. Again, the forgery was discovered and Laura apologised once more and left with the coin. Unbelievably, she returned to the same butcher's shop just an hour later and this time tried to buy some meat. The butcher's wife noticed that Laura looked anxious and was in a rush to make the transaction. The coin was said to feel 'very light and greasy' and was easily cut into three segments. Laura tried to make a getaway but was apprehended and brought back to the butcher's shop and given over to the police. She protested her innocence but her record spoke against her and she was given seven years in prison.

So serious was considered the issue of counterfeit currency that some women didn't even have to attempt uttering the coins to risk arrest. Sometimes simply possessing the coins was enough for a conviction. In 1866, 17-year-old Jane Holland from Sheffield was sentenced to five years in penal servitude simply for having counterfeit coins in her possession. Likewise, Ellen Marrs and her husband Thomas were found guilty of having fifty-two fake shillings in their possession at Brighton. They were given five years of penal servitude. Ellen and Thomas's two children were taken into the care of Warren Farm Industrial School. Ellen had only just come out of prison after being sentenced to four years in 1862 for uttering false coins, and had nine months in prison in 1861 for the same offence.

Individual uttering offences were minor in terms of value. The coins most popular with utterers were shillings as they were large enough to give reasonable change when tendered for drinks or food but not so large that paying for small items with them looked suspicious. Sixpence pieces, half-crowns and florins were also used but were either too small to provide much change or so large that paying for drinks with several half-crowns when good change had already been given drew attention to the utterer. As such, the average value of an uttering was much smaller than pocket pickings that saw jewellery and watches worth several pounds appropriated. However, as with so many property crimes, value was not a clear determinate of severity of sentence. The heavy terms of imprisonment and transportation that utterers almost always received were a reflection of a combination of assumptions. The coins utterers were caught with what were assumed to be just a few of many they had seen over the course of their careers. Considerable moral outrage was attached to this offence; prosecutors often implied that the offender had sought not just to rob an individual but also to defraud the state. To tamper with currency was an offence against England and the Queen herself. Coining offences remained some of the only offences during the Victorian period to be categorised as 'Royal Offences'.

Ann Lynch received her first conviction for uttering counterfeit coins in Liverpool in 1851. She was just eleven years old and spent five months in prison. The following year Ann was in court again, this time using an alias to try to hide her identity, and was convicted once more of having uttered a bad coin. Because it was her second offence and she was well on the way to being considered a notorious utterer, and despite being only twelve, she was sentenced to seven years' transportation. Ann never made it on board a convict ship, instead serving three years in prison. She was released in 1856 and returned to Liverpool, where she seems to have disappeared from all formal records.

Utterers worked alone or in pairs. Lone female offenders would usually be part of a network of utterers established by a particular coiner. Those who made fake currency might have a team of five, ten or more utterers who worked for them. Unless theirs was a very small operation, it was unusual for uttering to be done by those who physically made the coins.

Producing

The manufacture of counterfeit coins took place in every major city in Victorian England and with particular intensity in Liverpool, London and Birmingham. The materials needed – plaster of Paris for moulds, metal, acid and other chemicals – could be sourced easily and were highly mobile. Henry Mayhew described the process of making coins as simply as if it were a recipe for bread:

> Take a shilling or other sterling coin, scour it well with soap and water; dry it, and then grease it with suet or tallow; partly wipe this off but not wholly. Take some plaster of Paris and make a collar either of paper or tin. Pour the plaster of Paris on the piece of coin in the collar or band around it. Leave until it sets or hardens, when the impression will be made. You turn it up and the piece sticks in the mould. Turn the reverse side and take a similar impression from it; then you have the mould complete. You put the pieces of the mould together, and then pare it.

All that needed to be done after these steps was pouring metal from melted cutlery or similar into the mould and waiting for it to set. To coat the coin to look like true currency a solution of acid in water and copper wire attached to a galvanic battery would allow coiners to carry out the process of electroplating. Coins could then be made to look a little more used and they were ready for circulation.

The process of coining could be carried out virtually anywhere – not only in big urban centres but towns and small rural localities as well. Those who uttered false currency into circulation needed anonymity and a varied network of shops, pubs and merchants that they could use, so small towns and villages were not ideal. All producers needed were materials and privacy. Casting bad coins could be carried out in a backroom almost anywhere, making the practice hard to police and the culprits difficult to catch.

Kate Seager was arrested and brought to trial for manufacturing counterfeit coins for distribution throughout Portsmouth. Kate actually lived in a remote village outside of the town with two unidentified men who had been with her several weeks. Each was a notorious coiner in his own right. A noticeable flow of bad money into Portsmouth began with the arrival of Kate's team but the men escaped before police tracked the enterprise to the house. Kate was left to take the fall alone. She had been apprehended on her way back to the village pushing a cart that contained an electric battery and acids for the process of electroplating. In her house constables found batteries, nitrates of silver, gold crucibles and moulds. No actual coins were found upon Kate but the materials in her possession were damning enough for a conviction.

Producing coin was a convenient occupation for women. It could be carried out from home, meaning women with children could participate with relative ease, and even young and adolescent children could be engaged to help. Mayhew noted, 'Girls of thirteen years of age sometimes assist in making it.' Producers of counterfeit coins worked in pairs or small teams and divided the labour and time it took to make a batch of coins. Trust and discretion were an essential part of a successful coining operation so whilst associates might make coins together, teams might also include siblings, parents and children, as well as married or cohabiting couples. Depending on how the familial business operated, some members would make coins and others would distribute them. In family groups, adults could make the coins and send their children from quite a young age to distribute them.

James Carroll, from Liverpool, was known as the 'king of the coiners'. He had a criminal record that followed him to the city from his early life in Ireland, where he had also dealt in counterfeit coins. Alongside his wife, James had spent several long terms in prison for coining. His final sentence for coining came in 1890, when he was sentenced to ten years' imprisonment after he was discovered having made a series of poor forgeries at the age of seventy-three. The king of the coiners left a dynasty of royal coiners behind him. All four of his children were involved from early in life in making and distributing coins. Both his sons, William and James, had served years inside convict prisons. His daughter, Elizabeth, was sentenced to ten years in 1887 and the youngest of his children, Catherine, married a fellow coiner and was sentenced to eighteen months' imprisonment in 1890. The family were notorious within Merseyside and when Catherine was brought to court, the final member of the Carroll family to lose her liberty, the judge declared: 'It was impossible not to feel some sympathy for her inasmuch as she had been brought up in a family of coiners and had at an early age been sent into the streets to dispose of spurious money.' By making counterfeit coins and distributing them within a close family network, the Carrolls were able to retain 100 per cent of the profits, paying neither suppliers nor distributers. They had been able to make a living from producing coins for decades, living in respectable neighbourhoods and frequently changing the address at which they lived and operated, making them almost impossible to trace.

The nature of coining meant that successful conviction of coiners often required offenders to be caught red-handed at home amongst their materials. Disturbing coiners like Eliza Munns and her family was no easy task. Officers could face danger from boiling metal and acids that the coiners had readily to hand and were sometimes willing to use in order to escape conviction. Eliza Munns's house was raided by Inspector Brennan of the Mint authorities and a specially assembled team on Christmas Eve, 1852. The officers obtained entry to the dwelling by force and inside found Eliza, her husband, son and daughter actually engaged in making a batch of coins. Eliza's husband, Joseph, had a mould in his hand, which he attempted to destroy, and Eliza and the children followed suit trying to destroy as much as the evidence as possible. In the fireplace of their home sat a crucible and the metal needed for base coins. Nearby sat a galvanic battery ready for operation. A violent struggle between the family and the police ensued in which the officers' uniforms were damaged and eventually the Munns and the evidence of their activities were seized. Eliza spent a year in prison. Her young daughter was given a sentence of two months.

Your money or your life

The crime of robbery with violence is synonymous with men in masks stopping carriages on the highway and demanding of their startled inhabitants, 'stand and deliver: your money or your life'. But the reality of violent robbery in the Victorian period was not the stuff of bandits attacking country travellers. Robbery with violence was an umbrella term that might relate to several kinds of offence, from street muggings that used weapons or brute force to subdue victims to a case of pocket picking gone wrong in which thief and victim came to blows.

Robbery with violence came to the particular attention of the courts and press in the 1860s, when a few isolated cases of robbery employed the use of the Portuguese technique of 'garrotting' (or temporary strangulation of a victim) and sparked a national panic. The first half of the 1860s saw the most intense media coverage of this supposedly new and very niche crime. The garrotter was less gentlemanly than his predecessor, the highwayman. In the early 1860s it was lamented that the garrotter gave no warning, and operated with no honour. The *Hereford Journal* decried, 'Old times are gone, old manners changed'. For the garrotter, it was thought, 'despises all such courteous parley, and then first throttles you and then possesses himself of your purse, perhaps finishing up his attack with a stunning blow which shall incapacitate his victim from raising the hue and cry.' Garrotters operated in broad daylight, used violence even on compliant victims and were not the 'chivalrous, well-appointed' thieves of the previous century. Instead they were portrayed as ill-dressed and scruffy roughs, very likely former convicts. Editorials suggested that the 'highwayman of the Georgian period would not demean himself by such an ungallant bearing' on teenage victims, old men and vulnerable women, stealing valuables, clothing and even women's hair. There was, according to contemporary commentators, no deterrent for these violent roughs who knew that any detected offence would only lead to another sentence of incarceration, with which they were already well familiar. After a particularly worrying festive season in Yorkshire, the

Sheffield Daily Telegraph described the peril faced by every man and woman who found themselves at the garrotter's mercy:

> You walk homeward thinking mayhap of the bright fire, the warm slippers, the well furnished table the cheerful chirruping of the little birds in your suburban cage, and of the friends who are to share with you, this Christmas, the festivities of your home, and the next moment you are gasping for life on the road with one pair of hands in your pockets and another pressing cruelly on your throat. The one minute you are free from any shadow of suspicion and the next your arms are pinioned, a merciless wrist presses chokingly at your throat, a knee is driven with knife-like force into the small of your back and you are thrown helpless as a corpse on the ground.

Opinions of those who robbed with violence (especially garrotters) in the second half of the nineteenth century were damning. They were not the chivalrous gentlemanly thieves of decades past but strong and dangerous ruffians from the labouring classes: men with no honour, no morals, and no pity for their victims.

What the history of garrotting and other similar forms of robbery with violence have failed to show is that it was not only men perpetrating the acts that caused national panic in this period. Women, too, undertook such crimes. Whilst the strength and size of male victims made successful violent robberies by lone women against men somewhat rare, women were capable of attacking other women in this way and female offenders did, more than is commonly recognised, attempt these offences. Very often women were found to play a role in robberies with violence by aiding other so-called 'professional thugs' in their business. At the Manchester Assizes of March 1866, for example, twenty garrotters all faced sentencing for crimes that they had either confessed to or been convicted of. Thirteen of these robbers were men, and seven were women, meaning that roughly a third of the cases concerning robbery with violence at just this one assize session, in just one city, were perpetrated by women.

Reports of female garrotters tended to be largely the same. The women were usually painted as ugly, masculine and wicked – devoid, so it seems, of the typical gender characteristics other female offenders were still assumed to have. Female robbers often worked in pairs with a male accomplice or with a group of other women to accost unthinking passers-by or those weakened by alcohol. Whilst many individuals travelling through England's towns and cities in this period knew to be alert for the lurking male thug who sought to rob them, few paid much heed to the poor women who littered the streets, until it was too late. In London alone, cases of violent robbery were never far from the courts.

In 1862, Eliza Cooper, Mary West and Mary Ann King – 'all masculine looking women' – were tried for the violent robbery of Thomas Roach. After spotting him drinking in a Whitechapel pub with a large amount of money upon him, the women followed Roach as he left the establishment. Mary Ann King grabbed him roughly by the throat while Mary West and another woman held his arms, and Eliza Cooper removed the money from his pockets. The next year, Jane West and Elizabeth Gross – 'two repulsive looking women' – were charged with the violent robbery of Eliza Selby in Camden. Elizabeth Gross and Jane West waylaid Eliza Selby by asking her for a drink as she made her way to visit her brother. As Eliza made to move away, Jane West and Elizabeth Gross followed her. Jane West slipped a hand into Eliza's pocket while Elizabeth Gross came behind her and placed her neck in a chokehold. Eliza testified that this well-known 'garrotters hug' had nearly suffocated her. The two assailants ran off but were captured soon after by bystanders. That same month, Susan Light and her paramour, George Day, were arrested for a violent attack on a printer by the name of Myers. Susan was four months' pregnant at the time of the attack but was nonetheless the principal actor in an offence in which two men wrestled Myers to the floor while Susan kicked him violently and rifled through his pockets. Both Susan and George were sentenced to four years' imprisonment (their accomplice remained at large) but months after giving birth to her baby in prison, 18-year-old Susan died of complications from the birth. Much later in the decade, Mary Frost, described as a 'masculine looking woman', was charged at a London police court with assaulting and robbing Charles Carter. At around the hour of midnight, as Carter made his way home, Mary accosted him and seized him tightly by the throat while simultaneously removing a quantity of silver from his pocket. Luckily, Carter was able to detain her and hand her into custody.

Media attention towards robbery with violence subsided towards the end of the 1860s. The term 'garrotting' appeared less frequently in later decades, largely passing from the public lexicon. However, there is little to suggest that garrotting or similar crimes ceased to be an effective method for those wishing to rob. Indeed, despite the 1860s seeing a peak in reports and convictions for robbery with violence, there is nothing to suggest that the art of the garrotter or pinioning pickpockets was a new occurrence at this time, or that the crime ceased to be popular amongst thieves even as the twentieth century dawned. There were those who employed violence in their robberies by design, knowing that a strong hold on a victim or a swift blow to incapacitate them would lend ease and success to most thefts. Yet there were others convicted of robbery with violence where it seemed largely out of character when compared to their previous offences. Violence was sometimes little more than an unfortunate one-off in a career of crime otherwise typified by non-violent cases of theft and burglary. It is possible that very often, what was portrayed in the courts as a calculated robbery with violence, was little more than a regular theft from the person gone wrong.

Prostitutes were amongst some of the most likely female offenders to commit robbery with violence. The close proximity that prostitutes were able to achieve to their clients, and the vulnerable position that men in a state of undress could find themselves in made them ripe targets for physical restraint and violent muggings. Ann Farrell, a prostitute from Birmingham, was convicted of garrotting Bernard Churchill in 1866. Very early one morning as he made his way home from a night of revelry, Churchill was followed by Ann and after a short time she drew level with him and attempted to pull him into an alleyway. He tried to resist but suddenly found himself caught by the throat from behind by a male assailant. While Churchill was being held, Ann rifled through his pocket for money, which she then passed to her male assistant, who abruptly ran off. Ann was restrained by Churchill until a police officer came. For women like Ann, violent offences were relatively rare when compared to the pocket picking and robbing of indisposed customers, public order breaches and trading in stolen goods that typified most of their criminal activities.

In line with the sentencing patterns of the era, which saw typical penalties for property crime far outstrip those for violent and public order crimes, the perpetrators of violent robberies could meet with long sentences. During the height of public concern over robbery with violence, garrotters and others of their kind faced little sympathy from courts and would regularly receive between three and ten years in prison.

Catherine Bowden was born in Ireland but grew up in Cheshire, where she carried out all of her offences. She was reported to be the daughter of a 'steady, respectable, hardworking man'. From her late twenties, Catherine was arrested for a range of property crime. Some of her offences were petty thefts from private houses, such as the theft of a pair of boots for which she served a month in a local prison in 1878. She also worked as a pickpocket, stealing money, purses or jewellery from the person, serving from six months to a year in prison for each offence. Catherine also had convictions for violent robberies – one in 1879, for which she was lucky to just serve one year in prison, and another in 1883. (See plate 11.)

In these violent offences the man with whom Catherine lived would subdue the victims, whilst she obtained their valuables. In 1883, Catherine and her accomplice, Henry Brindrick, robbed a man named Frederick Hancock, taking from him his watch and guard. On the way home with a friend one night Hancock passed Catherine under a railway arch. She grabbed him by the arm and swung him round to face her and Brindrick, who struck him to the ground. Catherine then stole Hancock's watch and before he had time to rise, the pair were gone. They were apprehended and it was later found that Catherine's previous conviction for robbery with violence had also been committed with Brindrick, who had only just been released on licence for parole. Sometimes the pair would cut or threaten a victim with a knife; other times punches and kicks would suffice. Interestingly, while in court Brindrick employed the tactic of admitting his presence at the event, and even pled guilty to assault, but was adamant that he had stolen nothing. This was a calculated defence. The sentence for assault was likely to only involve a few months in prison whereas his eventual conviction for robbery with violence saw Brindrick given ten years' penal servitude. Catherine was sentenced to five years and released from prison long before her accomplice. In his absence, she returned to property offences that did not involve the use of violence. In 1892, Catherine received nine months in prison for stealing clothes and money from an unconscious Thomas Williams after she, another woman and Williams had been out drinking together. It was a crime of opportunity and convenience. In 1895 in Warrington, Catherine was held in prison for a single day after stealing ninepence from John Shoebridge. She had not accosted or harmed Shoebridge, but simply slipped her hand inside his pocket.

Catherine Bowden's mix of both violent and non-violent property offences show that for women, robbery with violence could be highly dependent on both the intended victim, the nature of the crime and, more importantly, accomplices. Bowden's case is one of many that illustrate that the majority of female offenders' crimes were not dependent on planning and previous practice, but on opportunity and circumstance.

What to do with stolen goods?

Women who carried out any theft or fraud ended up either with ready money to spend or with a haul of goods. Those with the latter had to find a way of turning stolen clothing, jewellery, household items and even food into profit. Disposing of stolen goods was not always easy. Some women were able to distribute stolen wares to the needy within their own communities but once outside a trusted circle it became difficult to know who would not care about the provenance of an item and who would go to the authorities. The safest way of selling on stolen goods was to use a disreputable pawnbroker who would ask no questions about new deposits, or a local 'receiver' who would buy and pass on the proceeds of theft. Here, too, women had a role to play.

Women who were receivers of stolen property were not necessarily engaged full time in the trade. They might be the keepers of lodging houses, beerhouses, or brothels that allowed stolen wares to be passed on or exchanged on their premises (see Chapter 4), or who made an income from a lucrative sideline in 'fenced' goods. Individuals trading in these locations could even arrange in advance with burglars and thieves for particular items to be procured. Certain pawnbrokers were amenable to taking goods they knew to be stolen. This was particularly the case in terms of those who ran informal or unlicensed pawnshops – or 'Dolly Shops' – that traded in second-hand clothing and shoes. On these premises, Henry Mayhew noted, one could find 'in the backrooms stores of shabby old clothes and one or more women of various ages loitering about'.

Women were perfectly placed to receive and pass on stolen items, because they were primarily those who acted as household managers and who sourced provisions for their families. In most working-class neighbourhoods women attending markets and shops, walking the streets with basketsful of shopping, were a common sight. Women were the most frequent customers of pawnshops. The commonality with which women bought and sold goods and bartered for domestic necessities meant that even when doing so illegally they aroused little suspicion. The destitute mother pawning children's clothing or boots was almost indistinguishable from the woman pawning the same items she had stolen. The nature of the pawnbroker's business meant that transactions were always made with discretion. Many pawnbrokers, both male and female, were happy enough to ask no questions of the customers who used their services; some actively turned a blind eye and let it be known that any goods were welcome. Property thieves soon became familiar with the business owners who were happy to take stolen goods.

The women that ran unlicensed pawn shops or received stolen goods in other locations were liable to prosecution if it could be proved they knew the goods to be stolen. Although proving such knowledge was no easy task for the police, if found guilty women would commonly face up to six months in prison or even a few years if it were a repeat offence.

Property crime: career or chance?

The cities, towns, shops and streets of Victorian England were as variable as the women who lived in them. During the period, there was no one single kind of property crime that women took to, nor was there a standard pattern of property offending that they could be said to have followed. How and why female offenders perpetrated property crime depended on all sorts of things: where they lived and what was around them; what their family and personal lives were like; if they had steady employment or experienced sudden crisis or financial strain; and who they were and what they were like as people. What we can be sure of is that property crime was rarely the sole method through which women made a living.

The Victorians liked to talk a lot about the 'career criminals' that stalked the streets in their thousands, paying for their nefarious lifestyles through crime.

Many Victorians assumed that both male and female career criminals did not and *would* not work. It was perceived that they simply refused to live within the law like everybody else. Career offenders were thought to be responsible for most of the crime that plighted society. In reality, women who resembled this stereotype most closely were only a fraction of all the total female offenders that went through England's courts and prisons in the nineteenth century. We know very little about them but because they existed largely outside of formal records (apart from criminal ones) like the census, and with such little information, it is difficult to fully understand why they ended up living this way.

For most female perpetrators of property crime, it was a temporary tactic. Robbery was something they fell into doing during a certain period of their lives, or a last resort that they relied upon only occasionally when times were particularly hard or employment was unreliable. Likewise, there was no set pattern to what kind of property offender a woman became. One woman might become a career coiner or housebreaker and only commit crimes of this nature, whilst another might steal from an employer when in service during early adulthood, pick pockets or pass false payments when money was tight, and even take to housebreaking if times became truly desperate. Property crime, primarily driven by need, could take place at any time of life in any range of circumstances.

A very dissipated woman

Sarah Watt was married to William Ainsley in Newcastle in 1850 and they subsequently had two children. The marriage broke down and they separated in the mid-1850s. William, an iron miller, maintained custody of both of the couple's children. It is not clear what led to the breakdown of the marriage, or whether this was a cause or a result of Sarah's offending. The timing suggests that Sarah began stealing as a way to support herself after she separated from her husband, and perhaps that crime was only a risk Sarah was willing to take after she had lost custody of her children.

Sarah's offending was concentrated in a fifteen-year period during which she was either offending or in prison almost constantly. In the ten years leading up to her final sentence of penal servitude Sarah had been sentenced to: one offence in 1857, seven offences in 1858, one offence in 1862, two offences in 1865 and three offences in 1866, as well as several other very short sentences. There were also a number of other offences, which carried terms of imprisonment from one to six months. During this time, Sarah was not known to have had any employment and appears to have made her living solely through theft.

Sarah carried out property crime wherever she could. Amongst her dozens of offences she was convicted of theft from shop entrances and doorways, stealing directly from individuals or from the houses and yards of her neighbours. Thefts from her neighbours were largely unsuccessful given her local reputation and easy identification. They were thefts of desperation carried out when stealing from shops was not possible or yielded no results.

The first detailed accounts of Sarah's crimes are available from 1859. At the beginning of the year, Sarah stole a pair of shoes and a pair of slippers from a shop and was given two months in prison. A few months later, she was brought before a magistrate charged with stealing 20 yards of flannel from the entrance of a shop. In April 1860, Sarah, 'well known to the police', was charged with stealing a pair of boots from a shop doorway. She also faced a second charge of stealing from her neighbours. Sarah was widely recognised as a thief and had been suspected as soon as the items of clothing were missed by others in her street. She was well accustomed to the cycle of offending and conviction and 'set up a random kind of defence' before pleading guilty 'in order to save herself going to the sessions' and thus avoiding a lengthier process and possible longer sentence. Sarah was given six months in prison. In January 1861, Sarah was charged with stealing a tub, the property of her neighbour, and given four months' imprisonment. Later that same year, Sarah appeared in court 'with her eyes blackened and her faced otherwise discoloured' where she had sustained a severe beating after attempting a theft. She was charged with stealing fabric from a nearby shop. By this time, she had been convicted nearly thirty times. In December of 1861 she was charged with stealing 23 yards of cotton from a shop doorway and received six months in prison.

In 1862, Sarah was still offending but she was also the victim of an assault. She had been living with a woman named Bridget Johnson for some time after leaving her husband. Sarah and Bridget had an argument when Sarah agreed to pay for some of the beer the two had been drinking together in the house, but refused to buy tobacco for Bridget. When Bridget threatened her, Sarah took refuge with neighbours in the same tenement. Two hours later, wishing to return home, she met again with Bridget, who fetched a hot poker from the fire and 'thrust it into her right eye'. Sarah was blinded in her right eye, and it was feared would lose sight in her other eye from the inflammation. Even as a victim in court, it was noted that Sarah was noted to be 'a very dissipated woman'. Sarah's reputation caused a lack of sympathy for her, and Bridget Johnson was sentenced to just three months' imprisonment.

There are no records for Sarah for two years after the assault. It may not have been practical for Sarah to offend during this period of recovery and readjustment as she regained the sight in her left eye. It was not until 1865 that Sarah was again apprehended after stealing a dress and a petticoat from a neighbour. It was noted that Sarah 'had not borne a good character in the neighbourhood' in which she had previously lived and as a result she was 'suspected of having taken the articles as soon as they were missed'. She received three months in prison.

In 1867, Sarah received her longest sentence yet – seven years' penal servitude for robbery from the person. She had approached a group of men as they stood together early one morning. As she stood talking with them, she was caught sliding her hand into the pocket of one of the men and drawing out his change. The men detained her until a constable arrived, and he found the money that was missing from the man's pocket upon her. Although this offence was not vastly different from the more than thirty others for which she had been convicted, a judge seized the opportunity to remove Sarah – a woman who had 'been going in and out of prison just as if it were home' – from the streets for a prolonged period of time.

Sarah's sentence of penal servitude passed with little event and she was paroled after four years in 1871. She initially went to a discharged prisoners' refuge in London, before eventually returning to Newcastle. The break that a long prison sentence provided from Sarah's cycle of theft and conviction does seem to have been effective. Although Sarah did not reunite with her family after her release, she did at least seem to stop offending. There is no record of Sarah after her release until her death in 1887 and to a greater

Plate 1. The murder of Nancy in Dickens's *Oliver Twist*.

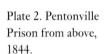

Plate 2. Pentonville Prison from above, 1844.

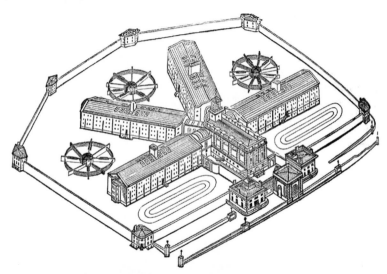

Plate 3. Contemporary images of Florence and James Maybrick.

Plate 4. Port Arthur, Van Diemen's Land (now Tasmania) during convict occupation, 1859. (*Allport Library and Museum of Fine Arts, Tasmanian Archive and Heritage Office*)

Plate 5. Hobart town, Tasmania, 1859. (*Tasmanian Archive and Heritage Office*)

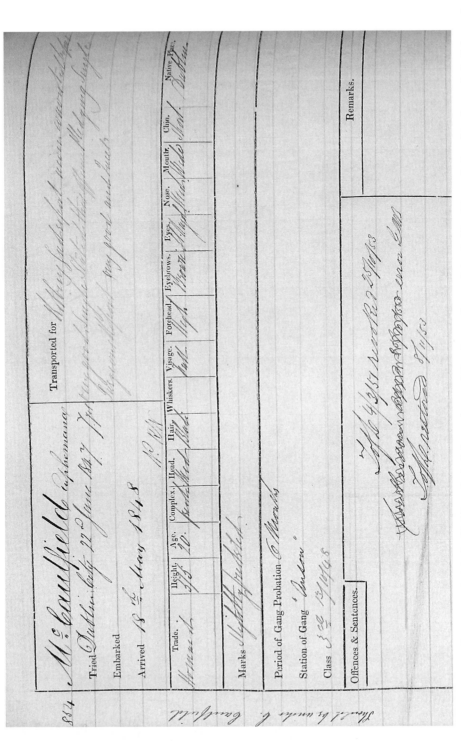

Plate 6. Conduct register for Euphemia McCaulfield, typical of the registers of female convicts arriving in Van Diemen's Land in the period of the probation system. (*Tasmanian Archive and Heritage Office*)

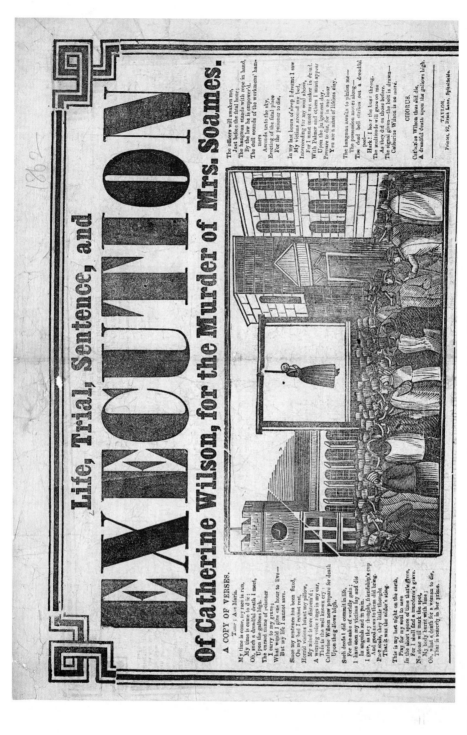

Plate 7. How the newspapers reported the life, trial, sentence and execution of Catherine Wilson for the murder of Mrs Soames. (*Courtesy of Historical & Special Collections, Harvard Law School Library*)

Plate 8. Mary Ann Reed, prison portrait, 1878. (*National Archives PCOM 4/65/11*)

Plate 9. Ellen Atkin, prison portrait, 1881. (*National Archives PCOM 4/60/24*)

Plate 10. Caroline Johnson, prison portrait, 1882. (*National Archives PCOM 4/63/19*)

Plate 11. Catherine Bowden, prison portrait, 1883. (*National Archives PCOM 4/65/23*)

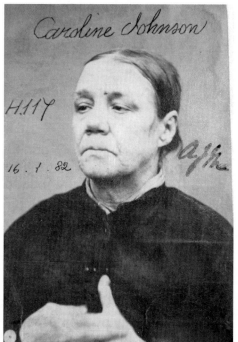

Plate 12. Sarah Ann Liddell, prison portrait, 1874. (*National Archives PCOM 4/60/18*)

Plate 13. Artist's impression of Margaret Walters disposing of Cowen's body, 1870.

Plate 14. Amelia Dyer.

Plate 15. Elizabeth Hustler, prison portrait, 1885. (*National Archives PCOM 4/67/24*)

Plate 16. Mary Morrison, prison portrait, 1883. (*National Archives PCOM 4/65/24*)

Plate 17. Mary Ellen Calder, prison portrait, 1877. (*National Archives PCOM 4/67/14*)

Plate 18. Alice Tatlow in later life in Birmingham. (*Reproduced with kind permission of the Tatlow Family*)

Plate 19. Prostitutes as depicted by *Punch* magazine, 1857.

Plate 20. Jane Butt, prison portrait, 1880.
(*National Archives PCOM 4/61/3*)

Plate 21. Jane Butt, prison portrait, 1885.
(*National Archives PCOM 4/61/3*)

Plate 23. Winifred Curran, prison portrait, 1883. Winifred was one of 'Little Hell's' most ruthless brothel keepers, with multiple convictions for assault and disorder.
(*National Archives PCOM 4/63/4*)

Plate 22. Rose Callaghan, prison portrait, 1883.
(*National Archives PCOM 4/68/4*)

extent it appears that after almost fifteen years of prolific offending she returned to a somewhat stable and ordinary life.

Thieves, robbers, swindlers and cheats

When it came to other people's belongings, dishonest women in Victorian England could be thieves, swindlers and cheats. Women's property crimes in Victorian England were more diverse than the stereotypes that seemed to have lingered longest in our imaginations. Women were not only cunning pickpockets and hapless shoplifters; they could also be dangerous robbers, child-strippers, hocussers and smashers. We know comparatively little about the full extent of female property crime, not only because a few well-known stereotypes have dominated their history but also because the more audacious kinds of property crime saw relatively few victims come forward. Crimes of theft and fraud were committed by women simply for the reason that a few minutes or a day of dishonest work could provide a better income than a week's or a month's wages in the menial and backbreaking manual work available to most working-class women. Others stole and cheated in desperation, stealing food and clothing out of necessity. Those who lost jobs, found themselves bereaved or abandoned by a breadwinner, or had unexpected financial crisis had no state safety net to catch them. Robbery, burglary, pickpocketing or counterfeit currency might have been the only means by which a woman could support herself or put food on an overcrowded table. There existed a vicious circle for those who had a history of property crime, which meant it could often be hard for them to desist. Employers were in no hurry to employ known thieves and this might leave even repentant women with few options for making a living wage other than to continue offending.

Chapter 3

The Brutal Side of the Gentle Sex

Violent Women

Violence was the last thing anyone expected of nineteenth-century women. These stereotypically meek and mild creatures, placed by society on a pedestal, were supposed to embody calm, passivity and obedience. Anger and physicality were masculine traits that had no place in the world of the home and family. Certainly, women only made up a minority of those convicted of violent crime in the Victorian period and acts of violence made up the minority of offences for which women were convicted. In the grand scheme of things violence was hardly characteristic of female crimes. Yet violent female offenders did exist to a greater extent than it may at first seem.

Although violence by women was thought of by the Victorians as an abhorrent rarity, the murderess was a popular topic for novels and plays of the day. Occurrences of extraordinary female violence sporadically appeared in England's courts and infamous cases of murder committed by Victorian women have remained a fascination to the present day. In recent years, author Kate Summerscale has revived interest in the murders committed by Constance Kent at Road Hill House in her real-life whodunit *The Suspicions of Mr Whicher*. The case of Florence Maybrick, found guilty of poisoning her Liverpool merchant husband James with arsenic-laced fly papers, has been causing writers and historians to debate for years and was recently tackled anew by Kate Colquhoun. Christina Edmunds, the chocolate-box poisoner, has a tale good enough to be the stuff of novels, and Thomas Hardy's Tess Durbeyfield provides but one of the many examples of the roaring trade still to be had in fictional Victorian murderesses.

For all their notoriety in fact and fiction the surprising truth is that cases like Kent's, Maybrick's or Edmunds's were comparatively few and far between when compared with almost any other kind of women's violent offending. Ordinarily female violence was not about poisoning or planning the elaborate demise of lovers for reasons of madness, passion or revenge. By far the most common murders, attempted murders and manslaughters carried out by women were acts of despair and desperation, perpetrated not against other adults but those they cared for the most – their children. Even these cases of fatal violence were small in number compared to the assaults and woundings that came to the courts daily. In general, violence committed by women was rarely fatal. Female violence was no less serious in nature than any other but often revolved around little more than the use of fists and feet, or whatever household implement came to hand in order to prove a point or settle a score.

This chapter gives an overview of the most common types of violence for which women were prosecuted. Amongst them are stories of despair and loss and others of anger and neglect. Together they show that violent women in the Victorian period should not be painted just as cold and calculating murderers or scorned and vengeful lovers. Violence was used by women in a range of situations under diverse circumstances. The only factor that seems to be somewhat constant is that it was unusual for women to undertake violence lightly. In most cases, attacks, fights and assaults took place when women felt there was no other recourse available to them. Violence served as a way of settling disputes, making a statement or solving a problem when women perceived that there was nothing left to lose.

Painful confessions of the wretched mother

In a time when women's primary purpose was suggested to be that of a marriage and motherhood, those that fulfilled one but not the other of these roles could meet with a mix of consequences. Married women who were unable to have children became objects of shame and pity whereas unmarried women who gave birth could face far more serious repercussions. Unmarried mothers attracted not only scorn and moral outrage; they could also face severe financial and social difficulties. Victorian England was a place in which extra-marital sex could cost a woman everything.

In Victor Hugo's aptly named *Les Miserables* (first published in 1862), the birth of Fantine's illegitimate daughter Cosette is ultimately her downfall.

Cast out from society as a fallen woman for having a child out of wedlock, Fantine is forced to use every penny she earns for the upkeep of her daughter when the child's father abandons her almost immediately. The reality of supporting a child alone in a hostile society led in fairly rapid succession to Fantine's dismissal from work, destitution, prostitution, ruin and death. The characters in Hugo's world-famous epic, like all fictional characters, are unrealistic vehicles that carry the sentiments of a greater truth. Sadly, though, in their essence, the experiences of characters like Fantine were very real for a number of women in Victorian England and further abroad. For mother and child alike the stain of illegitimacy could lead to disaster.

Infanticide was the umbrella term used for the act of killing children, particularly the murder of young children by their mothers. The stories of women accused of this crime all have their individual features and tragedies. However, the dozens of infanticides and neonatalsides (the murder of a child at the point of birth) committed by women throughout the nineteenth century share many similarities. Disproportionately, infanticides tended to be committed by young and unmarried mothers. Almost without exception, these acts of violence were committed by women struggling with social ostracism and financial difficulty.

Some cases of child murder were impulsive offences carried out by young women who had just been through the pain and terror of childbirth. Some of these women were either only recently aware of their pregnancy, or had been hiding the fact for some months from family or employers. Others did not realise what was happening until they were already in labour. It is hard to imagine the distress these women underwent, giving birth alone, usually for the first time, desperately attempting to avoid attention. In cases of neonatalside women experiencing panic in the immediate aftermath of childbirth might harm their children from fear of discovery.

Clara Humphries was just twenty-two years old when she was placed in the dock at Leamington Spa Sessions in 1872, charged with attempting to murder her infant child. Clara gave birth unexpectedly in the home of her employer, the Reverend Young. Mrs Young described that she missed Clara from her usual duties one day and eventually found her hiding in her room upstairs, where she had singlehandedly delivered a female child. Mrs Young heard the child scream and found it in a box wrapped in an old apron, with a piece of tape tied tightly around its neck. She obtained a pair of scissors and cut the tape, placed the child in a warm bath and called in a medical attendant. When Mrs Young spoke to Clara about cutting the tape, the girl, in a substantial amount of distress, said nothing but, 'Let it die, let it die'.

Most infanticides were not those like Clara's that occurred directly after birth. They were often preceded by months (if not years) of social difficulties, anxiety and financial hardship. Mary Newell's tragic story has much in common with those of countless others. At its core, her offence was a tale of misplaced affection and ruin. In her own words, from the dock at the Berkshire Assizes:

> I have known William Francis this six years. I have been in service since I knew him. I left Mr Ive's last August and came to seek for a situation, and going home I met him [William] in the street. He, knowing me, asked me how I was and if I would go and have something to drink. I refused it. By persuading I went. I was in his company some hours. He asked me if I was engaged for he wanted a wife, but did not want to marry yet, and his sister was keeping his house. When we parted he did not ask me my address or where I was going, I thought he did not care anything about me, only for his own ends. I stopped two months and a fortnight, when I was so unwell I was obliged to leave … when I came to Reading and told him how I was and asked him what I was to do (he knew I was in trouble by him) he said he did not know what I was to do, for he was engaged; he could not have me.

In her own delicate language, Mary had described her seduction by William Francis. The two had slept together after a night drinking in a local pub. William had hinted that their liaison might lead to eventual marriage but had either meant nothing by it but to charm Mary into bed or had changed his mind soon after. Months later, when Mary approached him for help with her pregnancy he turned her away. In January 1855, out of other options, Mary submitted herself to the workhouse in Henley-on-Thames. There she remained until she gave birth to a healthy son in May. After that, she stayed only long enough to recuperate before discharging herself in August 1855. From the workhouse, she went to Reading to confront the father of her child, testifying:

He was not in the shop when I went in there. His sister and someone else were picking fowls. I asked her where her brother was. She said he would be in in a few minutes. He came in. I asked him what he thought of the baby. I told him I wanted some money. I asked him what he intended to do and what I was to do. He said he did not care what I did; I could do as I liked; he should not give me anything. ... I told him I would swear the baby or have a summons for him. He said I might do so. He put on his coat and left me in the shop. ... I stood there till his sister put the shutters down. She said it was no use to stop any longer; he would not be back till eleven or twelve. I walked the town till twelve destitute for a farthing.

Women in Mary's position had little recourse when the fathers of their children refused to acknowledge them or contribute to a child's upbringing. Though Mary threatened William with a summons and a court appearance, there was no guarantee a bastardy hearing would end in her favour. She had, so a magistrate might imply, shown herself to be weak of morals by allowing the situation to arise in the first place. In a world bereft of legal counsel for the ordinary individual, or paternity tests, cases often came down to a mother's word against the suspected father. Unfortunately, the virtue and reliability of a woman who had produced a baby out of wedlock as a witness was often called into question. In many cases, mothers like Mary Newell were left alone to cope even after seeking help from the courts. Mary's confession continued:

I walked down the Forbury to the King's Meadow. I undressed the baby and laid it by the side of the bank, and let the baby roll in. Afterwards I walked up and down to see if I could see him come indoors. After that I went and got over into a field and sat under a hedge – it was in a turnip field – till morning, about a mile from Caversham. I went home on the Tuesday. I saw him [the father of the child] at Christmas, and he said he would pay for the child.

William Francis's change of heart evidently came far too late for Mary and their son. Mary was sentenced to death, which was then commuted to transportation for life. In the end, she served ten years' penal servitude in an English prison. In a rare turn of events, after Mary's case was heard and the court session closed, William Francis was hounded from the court amongst hisses and groans from an angry crowd who were outraged at the 'inhuman conduct' he had exhibited towards Mary. He was pursued through town, beaten by the crowd, pushed down a steep embankment and held down in a brook.

The crowd's extreme reaction to William Francis was unusual. In cases like Mary's, women only received a minimum of sympathy and understanding. Whilst the stories might elicit sympathy from those individuals that heard or read about them, little was practically done to help the situation of unmarried or destitute mothers. There were of course the disturbing cases of women suffering from what we now recognise as severe post-natal depression, or other mental health problems, for which little could be done. Sometimes stress, depression and anxiety over financial and emotional crises all combined. The cost of childcare and the inability of unwed or unsupported mothers to provide for such played a central role in a large proportion of the infanticide cases.

Sarah Jemmison was tried at the York Assizes in early 1857 for the murder of her son Joseph. Sarah's son had been born in 1854 and was placed with a Mrs Jane Marley, who lived near Whitby, to be nursed.

> The child remained there for a long period and the payments for its board were very irregularly made and an arrear of £6 or more having accumulated, Mrs Marley declined to any longer keep him, she being herself in a position in life too poor to support any additional burden. The prisoner was at that time living in the house of Mr Pearson at Egton, a farmer there, and in his absence at market she brought the child to his house. On his return he objected to it remaining there, having, as he said, as many as he could keep himself already. It was then proposed that she should take the boy to a relation in Moorsholm, a distance of 12 miles off.

It was December of 1856, and bitterly cold. As an act of supposed kindness the farmer did concede to let his own son take Sarah and the baby onto the main road with a donkey and cart. Sarah and her child were left at the junction of two large roads with nothing but cold and desolate farmland either side. Sarah began walking down one road that took her to a large tract of farmland. The child was not seen alive again. Three months later, a newspaper reported, 'a shepherd observed his dog feeding on something, and on inspecting it, found it to be the leg of a child.' The dog was eventually made to lead others back to the same spot where Sarah and her child had been dropped off months before and there the thigh and skull of a child were found. Marks on the child's skull allowed a coroner to deduce that head wounds had been inflicted upon the child during its life and were most likely the cause of death. Decade after decade, the same stories of destitute and desperate mothers graced the pages of Victorian newspapers and were played out in the courtroom.

Martha Hall, a 20-year-old domestic servant from Cambridgeshire, described as 'a sickly and not over intelligent looking girl', was charged in 1873 with the murder of her daughter Florence Emily Hall. Until March 1872, Martha had been working for her sister, and her sister's husband, John Adams, as a domestic servant. In early March, Martha was forced to leave her place in her sister's house after giving birth to a daughter by John. Initially, the child was placed with a nurse at the expense of Martha's sister. However, after two months, when Martha found herself another serving position, the payments stopped. Martha was now liable for the upkeep of her daughter. One Sunday, instead of going to chapel Martha appeared at the house of the nurse in charge of the child and asked to take Florence for a walk. She was not seen again until ten o'clock that evening. When approached Martha informed her sister that she had put the child with another, cheaper, nurse just outside of Cambridge. Her refusal to tell anyone exactly where she had lodged the child raised suspicion. Soon enough, a witness came forward and testified that she had seen Martha leaning over a nearby brook holding a child in her arms. The following day, the body of a child was pulled from the same brook. Well nourished and without marks of violence, a coroner determined the cause of death to be suffocation and shock. In court Martha made no attempt to deny what had happened, stating simply, 'I did it.' By reason of 'temporary mental derangement', Martha was convicted of manslaughter and sentenced to penal servitude for life.

Sarah Ann Liddell killed her son, Walter, after experiencing abuse at the hands of a lover and social ostracism within her village that meant she felt she had no one to turn to. During her court appearance, Sarah's tragic tale was heard in full and was reported as follows by the local press:

The prisoner was a married woman, but had been deserted by her husband, and for the last eleven years had passed her life partly in a domestic service and partly as an inmate of the union. About Whitsuntide of the present year she left the union with her child and came to live with her mother who occupied a small cottage in Cradley and was herself in circumstances of great want and poverty. There were also living in the house at that time a grown-up daughter of the prisoner and a man lodger named Meredith. On Tuesday, 28 July, the prisoner paid two long visits to her sister-in-law who lived close by, and appeared to be low and dejected. On the following day she was left alone in the house with her child, while the others went out to work. This was early in the morning; about half-past two the same day she was seen by a gardener 80 yards from the home, walking with her head down, and at very much the same time Phoebe Banner, the sister-in-law, came to her house to see the prisoner. On gaining admission by unlocking the door, she found in the room downstairs the hat, jacket and boots of the little child, and on going upstairs to where the prisoner slept she discovered the body of the infant lying dead with its throat out and bathed in blood. Close by were two knives, one large and the other small, and hanging outside on the staircase banisters dangled a rope. She gave the alarm and the prisoner was soon after apprehended. She was walking in a lane at the time about a mile and a half from the house, and from appearances about her had clearly attempted just previously to cut her own throat. She was taken to an inn and the wound attended to and on being asked by a woman if she was not sorry for what she had done she said she was not; that she 'was glad that the poor thing was now at rest in heaven, and away from the frowns of everybody.' On later occasion, when in the cells at Stourbridge, she repeated that she was not sorry and that she 'loved her baby' and that 'all sorts of trouble had made her do it'.

No witnesses were called for the defence, but the judge recommended Sarah to mercy, which she was later granted after initially receiving the death sentence. Evidence unearthed by the prosecution suggested that the Monday before the murder, Sarah was due to be married to a man named Williams. Just days before that, she had been induced 'by the jeers and abuse' of the lodger Mr Meredith and threats from Williams himself to go to live with him. The suggestion was that either Meredith or Williams was the father of Walter. The next day, the men turned her out of the house and they sent local boys to stone her. The prosecution and medical experts recognised that the abuse that Sarah had been suffering at the hands of both men, and her prolonged circumstances of poverty and want, had led her to the crime. Sarah was deemed to be 'in a low and depressed condition', which had led in turn to what they termed 'homicidal mania'. Although the precise nature of Sarah Liddell's psychological imbalance is unknown, it is clear that the attack she made on the life of her son was an act of desperation and distress. Perhaps most telling of all was Sarah's statement that her son was 'away from the frowns of everybody', which suggests some of the social repercussions experienced by unwed mothers and their illegitimate children – particularly in smaller communities. (See plate 12.)

Inhuman crimes

Whilst it was preferable that wives and mothers shun the world of employment to care for their families and domestic duties, for most working-class women motherhood had to be balanced with employment in the shops, factories, streets and pubs of England. The disparity between expectation and practicalities for mothers created great problems with childcare. This produced an opportunity for a select few women to capitalise on the needs of desperate mothers. Much childcare took place on a community level, with networks of neighbours or extended family members taking turns to care for the children of others. For those without such resources there was little alternative but to turn to professional nurses or childminders. The majority of such women took weekly or monthly payments in return for housing children. This service could be found in almost every locality and was common practice for women who could afford it and even those who could not (as illustrated by the plight of the mothers already mentioned in this chapter who struggled and often failed to maintain payments for childcare). Children entrusted to these nurses and childminders hardly lived in the lap of luxury. With a childminder making a profit from the money provided for care, the basic well-being of children was probably little, if any better from the enduring the impoverished conditions of many working-class homes.

Most childminders provided a fair service for a fair fee. However, there were those that sought not only to make a profit from providing care to the children of desperate mothers but also to exploit the situation beyond the confines of the law. The most notorious of these women were those referred to as 'baby farmers'. Baby farmers functioned, on the surface at least, like any other childcare provider. Some took weekly, monthly or annual instalments for the services they provided. Others would charge a large one-off fee or 'premium' (commonly from £5 to £10) in return for the informal adoption of an unwanted child. In this arrangement the child would be permanently given into the care of the minder and not seen again. The sums charged by these women were extortionate from the perspective of their clients although in reality they were rarely enough to pay for the adequate and long-term care of a child. Baby farmers might work on a child-by-child basis or else receive payment for several children at the same time. Children entrusted to baby farmers experienced neglect, violence, starvation and even death. Some children were disposed of immediately; others were neglected or abused over a period of time. Whilst some children survived and were rescued and eventually rehomed, infant fatalities were what often brought baby farmers to the attention of the courts.

The baby farmer was a figure who received more outrage and disapproval from the general populace than even those women who brawled in the streets or committed adult murders. Women who fought with their families, friends and neighbours were regarded as unfeminine and animalistic, but were not nearly as badly thought of as baby farmers, who were the antithesis of what Victorian society expected of women. The ideals of the day supposed that, above all, a Victorian woman would become an exemplary mother who was loving, caring and nurturing. The baby farmer, quite simply, neglected what she should nurture and destroyed what she ought to protect. Women committing the financially incentivised neglect of children could be found the length and breadth of England throughout this period. Urban areas, cities in particular, which allowed women to remain anonymous and move on with little interference, lent themselves especially well to the trade. The case of Margaret Walters was one of the first prosecutions of a recognised baby farmer in the Victorian period and remains one of the most infamous examples of the trade to date.

Margaret Walters (alias Willis, or Wallis) and her sister Sarah Ellis (or Oliver, as she was also known) were first arrested for their crimes in London in June 1870. The charge was for a single death, the murder by neglect of a small boy, John Walter Cowen, the illegitimate son of 17-year-old Janet Cowen. At the same time they were charged with the neglect of ten other children also found in their care, who when taken to the local police station were found to be in a 'heartrending state'.

Robert Cowen, Janet's father, had found an advertisement placed by Margaret Walters when he was looking for a place to send his daughter's illegitimate offspring. Margaret's advert had claimed that she wanted to adopt a child for the fee of £5 and that every other expense would be covered. A police sergeant followed the trail of evidence and, arriving at Margaret and Sarah's home, found the child, who was 'nothing but skin and bones, and was very dirty'. He also found:

> five infants about three or four weeks old all huddled up on an old sofa. They were all quiet and asleep. There were ten children there together ranging from about a month to about two and a half years old. Seven of them being boys and three girls.

The children taken from the house were found to be dirty and malnourished, and some had even been drugged with narcotics to keep them quiet. Their young age was a typical indication that the children 'adopted' by women like Margaret and Sarah not only failed to make it to adulthood, but rarely survived to the age of four or five.

Margaret and Sarah were reported as having been in business for about four years at the time of arrest. The pair took both monthly payments for their services and also one-off payments for 'adoptions'. The children that they took in were, almost without exception, illegitimate. In the time they had operated there had been as many as forty children in their care but no one could account for what had become of them. The adverts they had placed to gain clients were by no means unusual. Thomas Bassett, a clerk in the advertising department of *Lloyds Weekly News*, where the advert had appeared, testified to seeing both women on a number of occasions and that he had seen similar adverts placed in the paper for years by numerous different people. Twenty-seven advertisements that potentially matched Margaret Walters' handwriting were produced in court. One particular advert was read out: 'Adoption – a respectable couple desire the entire charge of a child to bring up as their own. They are in a position to offer every comfort. Premium required.' The price of the adoption was £4.

In court, Robert Cowen read out the following response he had received after applying to Margaret for the care of his grandson:

> In taking a child we wish to do so entirely, never to be claimed. We have been married many [years] but are without family, and have determined upon bringing a little one up as our own. My constant care shall be for the child, and everything which shall be for the child's comfort shall be strictly studied. Should you think more of this and will write saying where and when I can see you and how I shall know you, we shall feel obliged. We have had several letters, so are anxious to decide which to take. Yours respectfully, M. Willis

When the pair met, Margaret Walters was still very reticent to give her address to Cowen, explaining that she would not wish to be traced after the adoption as she could not bear to have the child taken from her after she had learned to love it. As events transpired her address was never given, nor was her real name. Walters came to collect the child from Cowen the evening it was born. She took £2 for her services and never returned for the other half of her fee.

Little over a week after Margaret took the child the police became involved and the full details of her business came to light. Cowen protested ignorance of knowing what would happen to the child, and claimed to be unaware that Margaret had other children in her care. It is impossible to ascertain the level of complicity any individual had in placing their child in such circumstances. An adoption that requires payment, a prospective adopter that will not give their address, name or any other personal details, and who intimates that a decision must be speedily made, does not seem the most trustworthy or legitimate option for childcare. However, it is not possible to know whether such customers realised or cared about the likely fate of the unwanted illegitimate children they sought to send away. Perhaps the threat of destitution, or desperation to avoid stigma and scandal caused all other considerations to be of secondary importance to the mothers and families of illegitimate children.

As Margaret Walters left Lambeth Police Court, to where she had been summoned to hear charges, a number of women who had been following the case approached her. They, it transpired, were anxious mothers desperate to know the fate of the children they had entrusted to her. Some demanded to know where their children were currently and what had been done to them. Margaret denied any familiarity with the women and then fell silent. Unsurprisingly, she was in no hurry to incriminate herself further by acknowledging the care of children for whom there was no evidence. She gave no detail of the other missing infants. Most of the women would never find out what had happened to their children although there seemed little alternative but to accept the likelihood of their demise. Mothers searched the details of the eleven children held at the Lambeth Workhouse after rescue from Margaret's house, hoping that they might be their own, but only a few would find comfort. The children in Margaret's care, it was said, were not named by her (so unlikely was it that they would grow up to need a name) but instead were known by a number. Some women demanded reparation for the money they had recently paid to Margaret for what now seemed like defunct services. A small court order of £3 was made for claims, but it was remarked that 'such persons who gave up children in that way did not deserve much consideration.'

The murder for which Margaret Walters was eventually sentenced to death was that of John Walter Cowen (see plate 13). It is estimated that up to twenty children died at her hands, with many more only escaping with severe neglect. Margaret's use of different accommodation and regular changes of name allowed her to escape detection for a long time. The very nature of the trade appealed to those who wished to disguise and disown the shame of illegitimacy and offered protection to women like Margaret. She was very possibly operating for many years before she came to the attention of the authorities. There will never be an accurate record of the number of her victims although John Walter Cowen was certainly her last. In 1870, Walters was hanged in prison and buried in an unmarked grave. Her sister and partner in crime, Sarah Ellis, served only eighteen months in prison for deception and fraud. Evidence only allowed her to be convicted of obtaining money from desperate mothers by false pretences. After she was released from prison it is not known where she went, what name she took, or by what trade she made a living.

It was at the close of the nineteenth century that this terrible trade in misery and neglect had its most famous case. The Reading baby farmer, Amelia Dyer, was convicted of the murder of Doris Marmon in 1896 but it is estimated that the potential victims of her baby farming over a period of decades could number in the hundreds. Amelia Dyer is, without doubt, the most noted and reviled baby farmer in history and has had a number of books devoted to her life and crimes. Her trial and the coverage of her case were sensational and have contributed over time to her transcending regular history to become almost an urban legend. (See plate 14.)

The practice of taking money for the care of children and disposing of them one way or another shortly after was not confined to the famous and extraordinary such as Margaret Walters and Amelia Dyer. The plethora of wanted advertisements in any Victorian newspaper suggests that the crime was far more prominent than criminal records would suggest. The legion of low-key examples of women undertaking this crime and overseeing the demise of a handful of children over a career is probably far more representative of the business as a whole.

'One of the worst offences known and practised in this country'

Just like baby farmers, women who turned their hands to providing illegal abortions were also considered to be not just violent offenders but the absolute corruption of womanhood. Rather than creating life as was women's God-given provenance, abortionists helped to destroy it. Instead of protecting and nurturing infants, they prevented them from coming into being. Women who provided abortions were painted by the courts and press as an abomination.

Male surgeons and chemists were often those that offered the means of abortion. Because medicine as a profession was only open to men in the Victorian period it was they who had the resources and training to provide the safest and most effective medical treatments. Yet, it could be difficult for ordinary women to have the social network or knowledge of which doctors to approach (asking the wrong doctor could end in arrest) not to mention that the services of doctors were beyond the financial means of many poorer women. The cost of a chemist's potion or the ability to hire a surgeon was simply too expensive. In these circumstances, local women with no formal qualifications turned their hand to midwifery and abortions. Procedures were carried out in back rooms with only the most rudimentary and poorly sanitised equipment. Despite best intentions held by those who offered to carry out abortions the procedures carried great risks to the women who underwent them. If an illegal abortion went wrong a patient could pay with her health, long-term fertility, or even her life. If discovered, the abortionist could face trial for wounding or, occasionally, murder.

Due to the nature of the abortionist's work it is as difficult for historians as it was for the authorities to identify women who either sought this procedure or carried it out. Women who had chosen to go through a dangerous, traumatic and illegal operation were in no hurry to broadcast their experiences publically. The accounts of the work of female abortionists that we do have are limited and are usually extreme examples of the trade in which grave injury or even death occurred. Even these cases illustrate that those who worked as abortionists were little more than ordinary women who, to most extents, were indistinguishable from their neighbours. Only occasionally were abortionists shrewd businesswomen who derived a living solely from the practice. Most were women who might work informally within their communities as midwives helping to deliver the children of local women or those who knew the pain and problems caused by childbirth first-hand.

When given the opportunity to look closely at examples of female abortionists, even those whose procedures ended in tragic circumstances, we might see women who were not monsters, but mothers themselves.

Elizabeth Ann Hustler was tried at the Leeds sessions in 1885 for having used 'a certain instrument to procure the miscarriage of a certain woman, namely Elizabeth Edwards, then being with child, at Bradford'. At her trial the judge noted that the victim was still in a very precarious state and that if her condition worsened, Elizabeth Hustler would be called back to face a murder trial.

In July of that year, finding herself with an unwanted pregnancy, Elizabeth Edwards had approached Elizabeth Hustler and placed 'great pressure' on her to carry out the procedure. Hustler saw Edwards several times and used a syringe and unidentified liquid to effect a miscarriage. Edwards had known to approach Hustler to ask for the procedure and at the trial the judge stated himself to be 'perfectly satisfied that she [Hustler] was an old hand at the practice'. The judge labelled abortion 'one of the worst offences known and practised in this country'. Without any defence Elizabeth Hustler was sentenced to six years of penal servitude. She served one year before being released on parole. (See plate 15.)

In 1885, at the time of conviction, Elizabeth Hustler had never been in trouble with the law before. She had no criminal record and no accounts of deviant behaviour – for drunkenness, brawling, assault or anything else. The police collected information on Elizabeth that stretched back twenty years and nothing could be found against her character. Friends, family and previous employers all testified that Elizabeth was honest, respectable, industrious and sober. Seemingly, her offence had arisen from nowhere. Elizabeth, however, had her own experience of unplanned pregnancy, which may go some way to explaining why she became involved in such a dangerous and illegal practice.

Elizabeth was born in Bradford in the 1840s. The Hustler family was a poor but respectable one, with four children. By the time she was twenty, Elizabeth was still at home with her parents but earning her own living as a dressmaker – a trade that she would continue for most of her adult life. Disaster struck Elizabeth in 1866 when she gave birth to an illegitimate daughter, named Benina, whose father is not known. As the cases of infanticide already mentioned perhaps indicate, no matter how much a child was wanted, loved or well cared for, unplanned pregnancies and illegitimate children were incredibly problematic for women in Victorian England. As well as placing a financial burden upon mothers and their families an illegitimate child could also make forming new relationships, future marriage and even finding employment difficult for unmarried mothers. These were issues that Elizabeth no doubt became aware of in the following decade, during which she raised her daughter and remained living with her parents as her other siblings grew up and moved on to start families in homes of their own.

As events transpired, Elizabeth and Benina's lives seem to have been largely happy ones. The year her mother was imprisoned, Benina married and she went on to have several children. Benina and her family moved to Canada in the 1890s. Elizabeth joined them a few years later, and remained living with her daughter and grandchildren until her death in 1926. Elizabeth never returned to prison and she does not appear to have gained another conviction. Whether she continued to provide abortions is unknown.

How Elizabeth obtained the knowledge to begin practising abortion is not clear. For many women, information relating to sex, childbirth and prevention of pregnancy was passed down through family and friendship groups. The time when Elizabeth began operating as an abortionist is also a mystery. A trade that relies upon cautious word of mouth seldom leaves a paper trail. There were of course those who carried out more exploitative and slap–dash procedures than others, and those that sold dangerous concoctions to desperate young women with no knowledge of their actual effectiveness. However, when it came to abortionists, charlatans seem to have been rare. Whatever the details of her practice, it is not difficult to see how women like Elizabeth could come to sympathise with the plight of the women they served. Those that sought illegal abortions were not only unwed expectant mothers or adulterous women desperate to avoid a scandal; they were also the mothers of large families looking to avoid another exhausting pregnancy or hungry mouth to feed. The work of abortionists was illegal but very much wanted by those who sought their skills. As Elizabeth's experience indicates, women were willing to go to great lengths to persuade others to help them procure a miscarriage.

The limited nature of what we know about midwifery and abortion in this period makes it difficult to assume or generalise too much from Elizabeth's case. Perhaps the reason we have so little evidence about this kind of offence, or the women that perpetrated it, is because they were not the heartless monsters that slotted easily into Victorian narratives of women and crime. They were rather ordinary women living largely unremarkable lives and becoming only occasionally involved through their work in the scandals and problems that the rest of society seemed unwilling to face.

A number of notable violent crimes committed by women were against children. What receives less attention is the fact that women in the Victorian period were as capable of using violence against other adults as their male counterparts. The assaults perpetrated by women ranged from the serious to the relatively harmless. The motivations, circumstances and forms of this violence were legion. Violent clashes with other adults were about enacting vengeance, sending a message, punishing wrongdoing or settling disputes over money, insults or affairs of the heart.

A woman's revenge

Throwing or 'casting' corrosive fluid was a surprisingly common offence amongst women and one of the violent crimes that required the most premeditation. Women planned to maim their victims in advance usually in cases of infidelity, suspected adultery or disappointed hopes of marriage. Victims of this kind of violence could be male or female. Sulphuric acid, otherwise known as 'oil of vitriol', and hydrochloric acid were commonplace enough that anyone might easily procure a bottle from a chemist as they were used in many manual trades, and even diluted for basic cleaning tasks. They were also the substances most often used in this kind of attack. Women turned to wounding others with acid most commonly when romantic relations between them and a man came to trouble. Women might turn to the use of acid to punish an unfaithful partner, or one that had cast them aside or mistreated them, or even to maim a love rival.

Mary Ann Breedon was a dressmaker who lived in the back streets of Birmingham. Like thousands of others who lived in the shadow of the city's factories, Mary Ann lived a hard but mostly ordinary life navigating the pitfalls of poverty. By the early 1870s, Mary Ann and her husband had been lodging in the house of her widowed friend Elizabeth Hughes. At the beginning of the arrangement Mary Ann and Elizabeth were, by all reports, on friendly terms. At sometime during her stay, Mary Ann began to believe that certain improprieties were occurring between her husband and Elizabeth. Unpleasant words were exchanged between the two women on the matter. One evening, Elizabeth returned home to the house to find Mary Ann standing in the front room clutching a small bottle of hydrochloric acid (which her husband often used in the course of his work). Fearing that her friend Mary Ann was contemplating suicide over thoughts of an unfaithful husband, Elizabeth advised Mary Ann to put the bottle down. Instead of heeding the advice, Mary Ann instead drew the cork from the bottle and threw the contents into Elizabeth's face. Elizabeth was badly burned on her face, especially around her eyes. By chance rather than design, none of the liquid reached her eyes but a surgeon testified that had this been the case, Elizabeth would certainly have been permanently blinded. Mary Ann tried to convince the court that the serious damage to Elizabeth's face had been caused by the accidental upsetting of the bottle. She was convicted but received just ten months in prison.

Prior to wounding Elizabeth, Mary Ann had no known offences and was not notorious for violent conduct or an uncontrollable temper. In fact, so ordinary was her existence that very little is evident about her life before she attacked Elizabeth Hughes or afterwards. Subsequent to her discharge from prison in 1874, Mary Ann was able to return to live in the same street she had lived in before her arrest. Here she faded back into obscurity. There are no further criminal records relating to her. The very violent attack on Elizabeth seems to have come largely out of nowhere. It was not the culmination of a string of attacks or an act by an individual with a history of violent offending. The attack was a completely isolated incident. The wounding of Elizabeth Hughes is indicative of the role violence could play in relationships between women. In this particular case the violence was intended to cause long-lasting damage and was not designed to merely chastise her for inappropriate conduct with another woman's husband or 'pay her back' for the pain this had caused. Mary Ann intended not just to harm Elizabeth, but to disfigure her. This took away Elizabeth's ability to attract men and inflicted on her a permanent punishment for her transgression. Simultaneously, Mary Ann was able to make a very public and serious statement to others of the consequences of betraying her in such a way.

Mary Ann Breedon's case was far from unique. Very few women who used corrosive fluid to harm others were repeat offenders, and if they were, the use of corrosive fluid was not a tactic often repeated. The casting of acid was used singularly as a reaction to a specific grievance against a particular individual. The 1890s saw a particular spate of prosecutions for this offence.

In 1892, Ellen Giles, a local of Lambeth, London, was charged with an assault of this nature on Charles Goodson, with whom she had been living. The two had cohabited as husband and wife in Brixton for about three years.

Goodson claimed that he returned home one Sunday evening and went to their bedroom to rest. Shortly after, Ellen came into the room where he lay and drunkenly began to accuse him of infidelity. She then retrieved a bottle from a nearby drawer and flung the contents over his face and head. Goodson rushed downstairs to try to wash off the fluid, but was so badly burnt he was taken to hospital so that a surgeon might treat him.

Ellen did not deny that she had committed the offence. Unashamed, she suggested that her revenge on Charles Goodson had been a long time coming. When arrested, a constable reported that Ellen stated, 'Yes, I did it; and I wish I had killed him.' She testified:

On the Sunday we drank together; I had some four ales, and you had some port wine. You have given me fourteen black eyes in less than six months. You have brought this all on yourself. You have come at night and annoyed me with your drunken fits; was a woman to stand all this and say nothing?

In her own defence she stated, 'He treated me very badly, and I could not stand it any longer: I meant to take it myself, only he annoyed me, and I did do it then.' It was felt that Ellen had been greatly provoked because of her treatment by Charles, and she was given nine months' hard labour.

In 1891, Private James McIntosh of Hulme, Manchester, had a narrow escape when an enraged Sarah Ann Clegg came to the barracks furious with him over a failed promise of marriage. Words passed between them and a dissatisfied Sarah then removed a bottle from the basket she carried and hurled it towards McIntosh. He ducked and managed to avoid it, and the bottle smashed on the pavement of the barracks yard. He testified that 'a strong sulphuric vapour was emitted from the bottle' and the pavement was slightly damaged. With little evidence about the contents of the bottle and no wounds to show, Sarah Ann Clegg could only be bound over to keep the peace for six months.

In 1895, Caroline Bucknell found herself in court over a classic case of lover's vengeance. Under the title 'A Woman's Revenge' the *Lincolnshire Echo* reported that Bucknell, a cook, and Frederick Gaskin, an omnibus conductor on the Old Kent Road, were sweethearts. The two had engaged in pre-marital sex on the understanding that Frederick had asked Caroline to marry him. Finding herself pregnant Caroline confronted Gaskin and asked him to push forward their plans to wed. Unfortunately, Gaskin had no choice but to confess to already being married to another woman. Days later, Caroline went back to find Gaskin and threw vitriol on him with intent to do grievous bodily harm.

Lucy Furniss and her husband lived in Poplar. In 1899, a quarrel between them arose after a heated discussion between Lucy's husband and their lodger, Charles Regan. The inference was that there were accusations of Lucy's adultery with the lodger. Infuriated at the accusation of impropriety Lucy went to Charles's room and threw 'a quantity of spirits of salts' in his face, seriously burning his eyes.

The casting of corrosive fluid was a statement of intent. The target was to cause pain and disfiguration as a punishment. However, practically, it was difficult in advance of the act itself to plan how much damage would be done to one's victim. It was not always possible to measure the strength of the fluid that the women had obtained. Some of those wishing to cause severe and permanent damage might find the solution they used caused irritation and discomfort, which healed soon enough. Others might find that what was supposed to simply convey a message could result in a fateful ending. Mary M'Kelvey was found guilty of the murder of William Martin, a sheriff's officer, in London. Mary was the daughter of the landlord of the Rising Sun public house and William was a regular customer. There were hints but no confirmation that the two had been involved in a sexual relationship. The pair had been talking together in the bar when Mary threw a cup of liquid into William's face. The solution was so strong that it caused extreme pain, instant blindness and William's eventual death, and also seriously damaged the bar on which it landed. Even Mary was burned by small splashes that rebounded onto her as she threw the liquid.

Of course, the use of acid, or other damaging fluids, to punish and disfigure was also a tactic used by men against women. This might be in cases of domestic abuse, when men's advances were spurned, or when they felt women had interfered in their personal, familial or financial business. Ann Hove was convicted of throwing corrosive fluid over her husband, but stated that it was her husband who had procured the liquid and raised his hand to pour the contents onto her. Luckily, she claimed, she had been able to knock his hand away and as a result, he had instead doused himself and sustained burns to the arms, face, mouth and right eye.

For such a dangerous and premeditated violent offence, the casting of corrosive fluids was not one that carried a particularly heavy sentence. Severe punishment only seemed to occur in cases that caught the popular imagination. Outrages like the wounding of police officers or the maiming of respectable women by jilted lovers made headlines and were likely to see offenders spend more lengthy sentences in prison. For the common street assaults between warring neighbours or rowing lovers, perpetrators could be back in their homes and communities after only a few months.

Only in cases where the violence inflicted by acid was so disproportionate to the perceived transgression of the victim were women likely to feel the full force of the law. One of the rare cases of casting that saw a woman receive a substantial prison sentence in the era involved Mary Morrison, from Manchester. Forty-year-old Mary and her husband Christopher had been separated for some time. Like many couples that no longer wished to cohabit, but who had no access to formal divorce, the Morrisons lived separately, but Christopher still made regular payments towards Mary's upkeep. One afternoon in the summer of 1883, a drunken Mary went to Christopher's workplace to demand her weekly allowance. With wages not due until later in the week Christopher promised that she would have the money within a day or two. Mary was not satisfied with the answer and produced, from under her shawl, a jug of undiluted sulphuric acid. She threw the acid at her husband, shouting, 'Take that, you blind b----, it'll make you worse than you are', and then left. Christopher, who already had poor eyesight, was virtually blinded during the attack and sustained severe burns to his face and body, too. Perhaps it was because the judge perceived Christopher to have done so little to 'provoke' his wife, because his wounds were so serious, or because this episode of casting acid did not fit the usual circumstances of seduction, jealousy and betrayal, that Mary was given a heavy custodial sentence and served three years in prison. Mary was one of only a few dozen women throughout the Victorian period that received heavy sentences for assaults with acid. (See plate 16.)

The use of acid by women was a relatively extraordinary form of violence. More often for female offenders crimes of violence were of a more mundane nature. Other kinds of assaults and wounding took place over affairs of the heart but also because of disputes over resources, perceived insults or neighbourly slights. Unlike the use of acid, most assaults occurred with little prior planning and saw women using their fists, feet, or whatever came readily to hand. Violent disputes between women and their friends, family and neighbours took place across England throughout the Victorian period. Whilst circumstances mattered more than location, cities and large towns were particular hotspots for violence amongst neighbours. Crowded slums saw families living cheek by jowl with scores of other poor families in residential arrangements where personal space and privacy were minimal.

At the beginning of February 1860, Elizabeth Seddon, 'a young woman of masculine appearance', was charged at Liverpool Police Court with having committed a violent assault upon Mary Ann Connell. Mary Ann testified that she was walking along the street with a basketful of clothes when Elizabeth attacked her. Elizabeth struck her several times in the face and then elsewhere on her body. Elizabeth Seddon had been due to marry Mary Ann's half-brother, but disapproving of the match, Mary Ann was said to have circulated a rumour that Elizabeth was a woman of 'loose character'.

The following week, Eliza Nelson appeared at the same court. She was noted by a newspaper to be 'an inmate of the workhouse who was said to be a most dangerous character and had previously been imprisoned for assaulting people in the house'. Eliza was charged with assaulting Ellen Lawler, a nurse, and a Miss Morton, who also worked in the workhouse hospital ward. What started as a disagreement in which Eliza told Nurse Lawler to 'go to hell' escalated when Miss Morton came to chastise her for her bad language. Eliza grabbed Miss Morton by the throat and tore her bonnet and dress severely. Miss Morton testified that the attack was 'a deliberate attempt to murder', which may have been overly dramatic as the judge was only moved to sentence Eliza to six months' imprisonment.

Days later, Mary Field was in the court charged with an assault on her elderly father, Samuel Breton. Samuel appeared in court with a bandaged head and stated that his daughter was 'the most dissipated character in Liverpool and was in the habit of going from one public house to another getting drink any way she could'. The previous day, Mary had come back drunk to the abode that she shared with her father. She proceeded to hit him over the head with a glass bottle, which shattered, cutting his head and eye.

Matilda McDonald was charged that same week in Liverpool with having stabbed a woman by the name of Jane Kilmore. Both women rented lodgings in the same house. One Sunday evening the two began arguing when Jane refused to go to buy ale for Matilda. Matilda responded by grabbing Jane by the hair and forcing her to the ground before seizing a knife from the nearby mantelpiece and stabbing her. Jane received injuries above her eye and to her arm as she defended herself. In court, Matilda apologised and blamed her outburst on drunkenness. However, the gaol keeper testified that she was completely sober when brought in by the police shortly after the attack.

Such violence committed by women was not particular to Liverpool, or the month of February 1860. The prosecutions related here were but a fraction of the cases that were heard, day in and day out, every year in the courts across England. Whilst the style and frequency of reporting on cases of violent women may have changed over time, the nature of this interpersonal violence changed little. Twenty, thirty and even forty years after the above convictions, virtually identical reports were still appearing in Liverpool and elsewhere.

In 1880 in Hartlepool, Kate Stamford attacked her neighbour, Julia Kenny, for stealing a half crown from her when Julia refused to let Kate look in her purse. Kate afterwards went to Julia's house to attack her. Kate hit Julia repeatedly with a rolling pin, a pair of tongs, a poker and then a coal rake, inflicting wounds on her head and face. She was found guilty of the offence, but was recommended for merciful treatment by the jury as they believed that Julia had provoked her into the attack. She received three months' hard labour.

In the same year at Portsmouth Police Court, Priscilla Comben was charged with assaulting two of her neighbours, Maria Humphries and Sarah Shanks, after a row in the local King of the Forest beerhouse. Priscilla, in return for her assault, was struck in the face by Sarah and had her hair pulled by Maria. An exasperated judge dismissed the entire case. Julia Carwley and Gertrude Gibson appeared in the same court almost a decade later, in 1889, for an assault on Alice Bardes. A lack of evidence meant that this case was also dismissed. In 1898 in Doncaster, Emily Cartledge was summoned for assaulting her sister-in-law, Mary Ann Cartledge. The pair had quarrelled after Emily flung a stone at her sister-in-law, hitting her in the eye. Emily was fined ten shillings.

The majority of female violence of this kind that took place in the towns and cities of Victorian England was committed by a small number of women who were repeat offenders. Most female offenders were not violent, but a small number found themselves caught in a constant cycle of violent disputes and reprisals with associates and local authorities.

A terror on the whole neighbourhood

Catherine Swift was born in the late 1860s to 19-year-old Irish immigrant Mary Swift and her husband James who worked as a shipyard labourer. The Swifts, like many other families surviving on highly casual and poorly paid employment, struggled for basic necessities. The family lived in Thornaby-on-Tees in Durham, and Catherine was one of their five children. Catherine passed an unremarkable adolescence before marrying William Barwick, another labourer from Stockton. It is not clear at what age Catherine's offending began, but it is likely to have been in her teenage years. Drunkenness, disorderly behaviour, bad language and violence between peers were all common in working-class districts of industrial areas. Residential areas like the one the Swift family inhabited could be popular targets for local police forces. By the age of twenty-one Catherine had already notched up several convictions and had a bad reputation with the police and local court.

In 1891, Catherine was charged with assaulting her neighbour, Catherine Reynolds, on a Saturday night. Catherine was drunk at the time of the assault and had followed Reynolds into her house before striking her in the face and knocking her over. It appeared that Catherine had threatened Reynolds several times previously. Catherine was given two fines – one for assault and the cost of the court case and another for being drunk and disorderly at the same time. Two years later, Catherine, along with her husband William and mother Mary, was taken to court and fined eleven shillings for resisting the police. The incident occurred when her brother Martin, a former soldier, was apprehended for disorderly behaviour and Catherine and the rest of the family attempted to intervene.

In June 1895, Catherine and William were charged with assaulting Robert Doran, the town crier of Thornaby. Doran was also a local moneylender and it appeared that Catherine was in debt to him at the time of the assault. When Doran called to collect part of the two-shilling debt Catherine and William attacked him. The Barwicks pleaded not guilty but were convicted on the strength of overwhelming evidence and ordered to pay a fine and costs of over £1. The likelihood of being able to meet this bill was small, given that even a two-shilling loan repayment had not been met. In lieu of payment, the Barwicks would have served time in prison.

The following year, Catherine again assaulted Catherine Reynolds, the neighbour with whom she had quarrelled five years previously. This time she was committed to prison for the assault. Superintendent Wright, who stood as a witness in the case, testified that Catherine 'was a terror to the whole neighbourhood' and said that a long list of similar offences could be proved against her.

During Catherine's frequent arrests and at least decade-long offending career she and William lived in a single dwelling with William's parents and his four siblings, brother-in-law and nephew, as well as Catherine's mother and three adult brothers. Life was cramped, impoverished and challenging. Limited funds meant that leisure time was largely spent in the local neighbourhood with a familiar community of friends and associates. Drinking cheap alcohol at home instead of in local establishments was a popular pastime. Drinking in nineteenth-century England was not dissimilar to the experience of drinking in twenty-first century England. Alcohol could provide entertainment but could also facilitate misunderstandings, arguments and violence, too. Often, it did not take a lot for friends out drinking to find that merriment and jokes spilled over into disputes and violence.

When violence was involved, it was not always the primary crime for which women came to the attention of courts and police. Violence could also be a product of a woman's arrest for another offence. Often, simple cases in which women were guilty of for drunk or disorderly conduct became violent crimes when the police intervened. Shortly before Queen Victoria came to the throne in 1837, law and order in England had been changed by the creation of the first professional police force. In 1829, the Metropolitan

Police replaced their well-known predecessors, the Bow-Street Runners, as the protectors of London's streets. Soon the old systems of militias and night watchmen up and down the country were replaced by other branches of this new formalised law enforcement body. Unfortunately, what, on paper at least, should have heralded an era of crime prevention and calm more often than not saw certain working-class communities pitted against police officers in an atmosphere of mutual dislike, distrust and harassment. Assaults perpetrated by women against the police officers who questioned or apprehended them made up a significant proportion of the violent crimes that saw women come before the courts. Women might attack an individual officer with whom they had a problematic relationship, or they might lash out at officers who apprehended them in the street or testified against them in court. Alcohol played a role in such a large number of women's violent attacks on police that it is difficult to separate the offence from charges of drunk and disorderly conduct. Female offenders and their violence towards the police will be examined in more detail in Chapter 4.

Unhappy homes

Domestic violence has traditionally been one of the most difficult offences for individuals to report as well as for the police and courts to tackle, and written records to document. Sadly, although society has come a long way in the intervening centuries, domestic violence still occurs and remains for the most part something that takes place behind closed doors. As an offence, domestic violence is difficult to address. History has shown that in the Victorian period, where violence was commonplace and personal lives were kept largely private, women could suffer appalling abuse within their own homes. Very often, for a mixture of personal, cultural and social reasons, victims of domestic violence had very little opportunity for legal recourse against their abusers.

In Victorian England, much as now, women were overwhelmingly the victims of abuse. They could also be perpetrators of domestic violence even though, in the nineteenth century, recorded incidents of female on male domestic violence were rare. Whilst actual rates of female on male violence are impossible to know, the fact that only a small number of abused men and their abusers made it to court was doubtlessly a result of the social and cultural difficulties faced by male victims of domestic violence. In many communities, husbands or lovers would have been ridiculed for being victimised by the women they lived with – the dominant perception being that to 'allow' such treatment by a woman was unmanly. For similar reasons, male victims may also have faced difficulty in pursuing prosecution or obtaining justice of their female abusers. Those female on male domestic violence cases that did make it to court usually involved working–class women who had used extreme violence. Middle–class domestic violence – particularly that of women against men – remained largely hidden from public view, and thus also from the courts, criminal records and history. To a certain extent the following domestic violence cases are exceptional and do not provide a complete impression of the nature of female domestic violence. Nevertheless, they can still give valuable insight into abuse by women in a domestic setting and offer the opportunity to learn more about the lives and personal relationships of violent female offenders.

Jane Alty and Henry Cushion were married in the Holy Trinity church in St Marylebone, London, in July 1861. Jane was twenty-one and marrying for the first time; Henry was a widower with a daughter from his previous marriage. Five years later, the pair were living in Putney. Although still together, their marriage was not, by either of their accounts, a happy one. Henry later testified that both 'had lived a very unhappy life from three weeks after our marriage.' Both Henry and Jane made accusations of violence, alcoholism, verbal abuse and poor financial management. According to Henry, Jane had sold his house and belongings and left him destitute. Jane had taken Henry to Marlborough Police Court upwards of ten times on charges of assault and had him convicted in 1864 for twenty-eight days' imprisonment after he cut her head. Henry maintained that her accusations were false. Henry himself had taken Jane to the local magistrates for running up large debts. Jane was bound over to keep the peace for six months. Henry further claimed that she regularly locked him out of the house and that he had lost much valuable business through her behaviour. He also hinted at infidelity. Jane argued that his accusations were groundless and that her husband had a vendetta against her, and that he would never be satisfied until he had put her in prison. Jane suggested that Henry 'ill-used' her, verbally abused her and left her to make her own living.

With any case of one individual's word against another, it is not possible to discern fact from fiction, or anger and spite from genuine grievance. What is clear is that both had been taken to court on the other's account and that Jane and Henry's was a violent household. Fierce disagreements over money, behaviour and responsibilities had characterised their time together.

Although the 1857 Matrimonial Causes Act made divorce available through court of law (previously the dissolution of a marriage had required Act of Parliament) the effort and expense of such a case meant that divorce was rarely used outside of wealthy and influential circles. Many couples who no longer wished to live as husband and wife would arrange their own, informal, separation. In amicable separations, women might be permitted to take their own possessions and begin a new life, but their right to do so was by no means assured. Women's rights to property remained largely within their husband's discretion. However, even if separated, whilst still legally married, husbands were also responsible for their wife's debts and maintenance.

In May 1866, Jane and Henry had been selling their possession with the help of a broker, with the intention of permanently separating. It appears that in selling off their belongings, Jane would receive half of the money upfront, and then receive maintenance from Henry after they ceased to live together. At about eleven o'clock after a night of selling Jane headed further into Putney and Henry went to their home for, in his own words, 'a doze with my clothes on'. When he woke, Henry's hands were tied above him and he was secured to the bed. He had been woken by the feel of Jane cutting his throat with a razor. The wound that Jane inflicted was serious. A member of the college of surgeons testified that 'it just escaped the main arteries', and if the arteries had been cut, he would have been dead within minutes. When brought to the police station Henry had been in danger of death from loss of blood. Remarkably, he survived the attack. Even more remarkable was that Jane made no effort to deny her part in it. She even accompanied Henry to the police station to seek help.

During Jane's trial at the Old Bailey, Jane painted a sad picture of her motivation for attacking Henry and what passed between them that night.

Henry testified that after cutting him, Jane had said, 'I will see you go away from me', meaning that she would kill him before she let him leave. Jane did not deny this, stating, 'I was very jealous of my husband, I did not like his going away from me I found I could not bear it.' Jane was sentenced to ten years' penal servitude, and was released on licence six years later, in 1872. There are no records of her having offending again.

The case of Jane and Henry Cushion can hardly be taken as a typical case of domestic violence. The level of violence that Jane resorted to was extreme. However, Jane's case does share several factors that seem to have been typical of female-perpetrated domestic violence in this period. Attacks on spouses usually came after years of marital discord where women had received physical or verbal abuse. The prospect of separation from a spouse, and concerns over financial stability, also played a role. Drunkenness was often cited as a primary factor in many of the cases of female on male domestic violence. Doubtlessly, some women guilty of domestic violence were labelled drunkards, with little corroborating evidence. The spectre of the female drunk provided a familiar and tidy narrative with which to explain female deviance. Yet more often than not, witnesses to assaults or records of previous convictions showed inebriation played a key role in violence of this kind. In many of these cases, alcohol turned disputes over household duties, money, fidelity and the rights and responsibilities into altercations of a much more serious nature. With inhibitions lowered and judgement impaired, serious assaults were committed on the spur of the moment, with disastrous consequences. Many of the men who prosecuted their wives and partners in court suggested that they had previously been victims of domestic violence, but were only compelled to come forward after sustaining serious injury requiring medical attention or after the police became involved. The small selection of cases that follow offer an illustration of the severity and nature of the kind of domestic assaults that women were prosecuted for in the period.

In 1875, Amelia Chester was charged at Lambeth for assaulting her husband with a poker. Mr Chester had returned home after a day working and demanded that food be prepared for him. Amelia declined to do as he asked and suggested that if he 'did not get her some drink she would murder him'. A frenzied attack followed in which Amelia attempted to strike him with a knife and then dealt him three blows with a poker. In court, it was ascertained that the attack was not the first that a jealous Amelia had made on her husband. Despite the remorse for her actions she had shown at the police station Amelia was sentenced to two months in prison with hard labour.

Forty-three-year-old Jane McDermott of Liverpool had been unhappily married to her husband for just nine months when, in 1895, she doused him in paraffin as he slept by the fire and set him alight. Jane's 'drunken habits' were cited as reason for their matrimonial discord. Astonishingly, Mr McDermott survived the ordeal, albeit badly burnt, and Jane received just twelve months' imprisonment.

Mrs Sodden from Gainsborough went on the run from police in 1892 after she made an attempt to murder her husband. Mr and Mrs Sodden both worked as hawkers (street sellers) – poorly paid work that saw many living below the poverty line. On the day in question, 'both being the worse for drink', Mrs Sodden and her husband were having an altercation when Mrs Sodden retrieved a knife from one of their hawking baskets and stabbed her husband in the throat before fleeing the scene.

In 1874, Mary Hawkins was taken to court in Stafford after stabbing her husband George in the thigh with a knife. A main artery in George's leg was severed and he had to be taken to the local infirmary in danger of death. Mary was taken into police custody. The only motivation for the assault was: 'A quarrel had taken place and the woman, who was under the influence of drink, struck the blow as her husband was leaving the house.' Mary testified to the police that her husband had inflicted the wound on himself. Mary's character was not in her favour as she had been convicted of drunkenness by the magistrate only the previous day. Quite remarkably, on this occasion Mary was liberated after paying the court's costs and on the promise of altering her behaviour.

The murder of a spouse by a woman was rare, both in cases of pre-meditated murder and in the case of fatal fights or domestic assaults. This was partly due to luck rather than judgement and to the size and strength disparity between many men and women. When deaths of this kind did occur, it could be by accident as much as design.

Ellen Kinsley was charged with the manslaughter of her husband John in 1887. Ellen worked as a hawker and lived in Leicester. On a Wednesday night in February of that year, Ellen had been intoxicated and arguing with her husband. She threw two cups at him, one of which rendered a large cut on his nose. John bled heavily from the wound all night. By the time medical assistance arrived the following day John had bled to death. Ellen was drunk when found by the police later that day and when the news of John's death was broken to her, she made no denial of her role in it. Ellen stated, 'Good job, too; he ought to have been dead long ago.' Little defence was made for Ellen when the case reached court almost three months later and she was found guilty of the manslaughter of her husband. Ellen served only six weeks in prison for the offence.

Recorded cases of domestic violence in which other adults were attacked by women, whatever the circumstance or outcomes, remained uncommon throughout the Victorian period. Female offenders charged with violence in a domestic setting were far more likely to appear in court for the neglect, abuse, manslaughter and even murder of their own children. Female offenders far outnumbered male offenders in cases of child cruelty, neglect and abuse.

Mary Ellen Calder had begun cohabiting with John Moss in Sunderland in 1876. Mary had five children of her own, and John was a widower with a young son. Mary had no former convictions for violence or any other offences. In the twelve months that the couple lived together neighbours noticed that John's child, George, was treated significantly worse by Mary than her own children. Concerned witnesses to Mary's treatment of George had often tried to intervene but to little effect. A newspaper reported:

> It had been very much neglected and ill-used; it had to go out and beg for bread from the neighbours, and every time it did so it was whipped severely by the female prisoner. It was kept without clothing, whilst the other children were far better clad; and on one occasion when it begged for bread, the female prisoner took it in and said it would be a long time before it got another piece. The child was not seen again for a month and then it was observed to be in a very bad condition.

When Mary and John had begun living together, George was strong and healthy but by December 1876 he had been 'reduced almost to a skeleton'. George died of starvation on Christmas Eve 1876. The coroner held that a healthy 6-year-old should weigh 'at least about 3 stones' whereas George was found to weigh less than half of that at just 18 pounds.

Both Mary and John were put on trial after George's death. No witnesses testified as to John's role in the neglect of his son but rather spoke of his failure to intervene. Mary and John were both found guilty of manslaughter at Durham Assizes in February of 1877 and sentenced to fifteen years' penal servitude each (see plate 17). The couple had no contact during their time in prison and Mary was released on licence just over nine years later. It is unclear whether the two ever met again or what happened to Mary's own children during and after her incarceration. Throughout her time in prison, Mary maintained her innocence, claiming that she had not intentionally harmed George and admitting only that she had perhaps been negligent of summoning medical help for him.

Cases of abuse and neglect were apparent throughout the nineteenth century. Reported and prosecuted instances of child cruelty became much more common from the 1880s onwards, after the establishment of several charitable societies that sought to protect children in danger. Societies began locally, the first such example being the Liverpool Society for the Prevention of Cruelty to Children in 1883. This was closely followed by a London counterpart in 1884, which by the end of the decade had become a countrywide effort that was renamed the National Society for the Prevention of Cruelty to Children. After its establishment, the NSPCC undertook many prosecutions on behalf of neglected and abused children. Women brought to court for the harm of their children could range from mothers using over-zealous discipline and stepmothers like Mary Calder who had purposely abused the children in their care, to others who had neglected to protect their children from illness and injury. Much like cases of women who committed other forms of domestic violence against their spouses, in incidents of child neglect and abuse, alcohol all too often played a part.

Emily Atkins was sent to prison in 1899 for the neglect of her 3-year-old daughter Clara. Concerns had been raised by the neighbours over the health of the child and when a warrant officer went to Emily's house to investigate he found her in her kitchen, where she had her child tied to a chair surrounded by dirty rags. The child was extremely dirty and her hair was matted. Her body and legs were black with dirt and bruises. Emily admitted that she had not washed her child for a month. The child's legs were so badly deformed by rickets that the divisional surgeon declared that they would need to be broken and set in splints in order to regain their proper shape. The child had also been badly burned when a pan of scalding water had fallen on her. Emily protested that this had been an accident and claimed that poverty was the main cause of her neglect. She had three other children and her husband had left home sometime previously. When asked, her husband claimed he would not send maintenance money to his wife 'as she would only spend it all on drink'. Emily had previously been punished for the neglect of her children and on this occasion was sentenced to a further six months of imprisonment. In reply to her charge, a newspaper reported that Emily had claimed 'she was much better off when she was in prison before and that it would be the same again'. Two years later, Emily was living alone and destitute in Greenwich Workhouse.

A Manchester woman, Margaret Nixon, was sent to prison for three months in 1874 for the abuse of her 3-year-old son. Margaret had been drinking with friends in Deansgate, taking her young son in tow. When the child began to cry Margaret kicked him and sent him sprawling across the room. When her friends chastised her she left, kicking the boy again out through the doors and onto the street. A concerned passerby reported Margaret to a nearby constable, who then went to arrest her. Margaret was unashamed, and in her defence of the violence she had used she suggested that she had merely 'pushed the child with her feet'. Margaret justified her actions by claiming that the child had 'annoyed her' by insulting her.

The gentler sex?

Throughout the Victorian period, violent crimes perpetrated by women remained the minority of female offences. Despite sensational reports of middle-class femme fatales and cunning lady poisoners stealing the headlines of the day, and continuing to make thrilling histories in modern times, these crimes were exceptional and not representative of the overall nature of female violence in the period. Female murderers were rare. The majority of female violence was non-fatal. The burdens of childcare fell primarily upon women and as such, women committed the majority of cases of child neglect, abuse and killing. However, records of women's violence against other adults, in which they lashed out and brawled over familiar issues of love, ownership and honour, were by far the most common kind of female violence. Many of the acts of violence committed by women took place at the same time as crimes of drunkenness and public order – to which we now turn.

Chapter 4

The Demon Drink and the Great Social Evil

Challenging Public Order

U nlike their relatively liberal predecessors in the eighteenth century, on the surface, Victorians were often careful to disassociate themselves from the pleasures of the flesh. We have since come to know that the Victorians were not as averse to sex or alcohol as they would have had us think. After all, the Victorians invented photographic pornography and had a legendary number of gin palaces, pubs and opium dens. As with any time and place, ideals and practice in Victorian England seldom came together flawlessly.

Whatever went on behind closed doors, it was felt for women in particular, that overt sexuality and drunkenness were two things that should never occur in public if respectability and reputation were to be preserved. The presiding moral sensibilities of the age demanded sobriety and chastity. Although not mutually exclusive, drunkenness and prostitution were tied together in social and legal consciousness as both the product and cause of immorality in England. Drink and sexual indiscretion were repugnant in their own right and posed a secondary threat by giving rise to crimes of obscenity, violence, disorder and damage. Whilst crimes of theft most often saw women convicted of felonies and sent to convict prisons and violent crimes stole newspaper headlines, women who drank excessively or sold themselves on the streets (often both) probably constituted the largest single group of female offenders in Victorian England.

The demon drink

Alcohol played a huge role in Victorian culture, just as it does in our own. Not only was drinking used to mark great celebrations or days of sombre reflection like weddings and funerals, but was also one of the main leisure activities available to the vast majority of adults in Victorian England. Cash payments to workers on Fridays meant that public houses enjoyed a roaring trade every weekend until the money was spent. Even those too poor to go out drinking could obtain cheap alcohol and drink it in their houses and yards with family and friends. Throughout the year groups of friends and neighbours would gather to drink in the streets and courts around towns or in village squares. For men and women of all classes drink provided entertainment and escapism. For the unhappy, or the bored with no other means, alcohol provided a solution, at least temporarily, to their problems. It was often quipped that for the desperate the quickest way out of most towns was a bottle of gin. The Victorian age was one in which concern about the rates of alcohol use and the perils of drink gathered momentum, too. The Victorian age simultaneously saw the birth of the temperance associations that urged the population to abstain from drink and the rise of inebriate institutions set on curing the disease now recognised as alcoholism.

Human nature has not changed so much in the last 170 years that the reasons people turn to alcohol are any different now than they were then. There were those who drank for leisure, and those who drank because of distress and need. There were those fighting unseen battles with addiction and mental illness, which contributed to a chaotic, desperate and perpetual cycle of drunkenness and detrimental consequences. Women who drank for any of these reasons or myriad others found themselves in court for offences that would seem completely at home in the late nights and weekends of modern-day England.

In 1898, Mary Ward from Croydon was charged for the ninety-ninth time with drunk and disorderly conduct. A local newspaper reported:

> She, as usual, denied being drunk, admitting however, having had some beer, but asserting that she had all her senses. A constable spoke to finding Mary outside the Croydon workhouse hallooing [*sic*: to cry or shout halloo to attract attention] and shouting at the top of her voice and surrounded by a crowd of about 150 persons. She declared that she wanted to go to the police station on the ambulance and the officer accommodated her.

Mary's arrest came just one week after discharge from Holloway Prison following a similar charge for which she had served one month in custody. Fairing no better on this charge she was given another month in prison. Shouting and causing a nuisance, making a loud public scene, might seem like a relatively light-hearted consequence of over-indulgence but Mary's difficulties and struggle with drinking stretched back some way to darker episodes.

The first recorded occasion of Mary's drunkenness was from almost twenty years earlier. In 1881, Mary was a resident of Mitcham, South London. She lived with her agricultural labourer husband George and infant son David. In August, Mary was charged at Croydon Police Court with using threatening language and being drunk. It was not Mary's first offence; police noted that she had been previously convicted, but perhaps it was her most serious breach of public order to that date. Two police constables had visited Mary at home to serve her with a court summons for a prior offence (most likely to also have involved drunkenness). Mary 'immediately tore it up and declared that she did not care for that,' ducked indoors and returned with a poker, 'threatening to kill everyone in the road.' Mary attempted to downplay the incident, claiming the poker was her young child's toy and that the police had ill-used her by tearing the clothes off her back and dragging her along the floor. The magistrate in judgement was not convinced and ordered Mary to pay a fine or serve fourteen days' hard labour in default.

In 1885, Mary was found running along the main line of the London, Brighton and South Coast Railway. When a foreman at the Mitcham Junction station called out to her she announced that she intended to throw herself under a train that was fast approaching from Wimbledon. The reporter noted that 'her hair was dishevelled and she was of very wild appearance.' Witnesses tried to intervene and one got hold of her with the train just yards away. Mary, however, was intent on ending her life and a 'fierce' struggle ensued. The line was busy and two other trains were approaching the station. In a scene worthy of any silent film, so hard did Mary fight with the man attempting to restrain her that both of them fell onto the tracks, with the train imminently upon them. Only by the quick actions of a nearby signalman, who halted the train, was tragedy averted. With much effort,

Mary was taken back to the platform and detained for the police. While waiting she made another unsuccessful attempt to throw herself onto the 'metals' below. Although she had caused a great deal of disruption and placed other passengers in danger, not to mention that suicide in itself was an illegal act, Mary was not charged. Instead, she was released to the care of her husband, who merely 'attributed the act to excessive drinking'.

With such dangerous and damaging behaviour it is surprising that Mary's actions were attributed to nothing more serious than indulgence in drink, especially when her only regret over the incident was that 'she was sorry she had not managed to commit suicide'. With apparently little comprehension of the deeper difficulties Mary was undergoing it is unsurprising that she did not receive the help that she clearly needed. As a result, Mary proceeded for well over a decade to perpetrate almost monthly episodes of drunken and 'disorderly' behaviour.

Five years after her suicide attempt, Mary was again brought up at the Croydon Petty Sessions. It was her thirty-second charge of being drunk and disorderly around her home town of Mitcham. She pleaded guilty and before official proceedings got underway, the magistrate candidly asked Mary to account for herself. She stated, 'I have been a teetotaller for three weeks.' Before she could continue, the exasperated judge reminded her that this was for good reason as she had been serving time in prison. Mary continued, 'I took the pledge when you gave me a month, and I wanted my husband to be a teetotaller; but he won't and I got into trouble. I found him at the Three Kings last night and had some beer.'

At twenty-past one that morning Mary had gone to the police station, very drunk, and had asked to be locked away. She refused to leave when asked to and became so disorderly that her request was eventually granted. The magistrate was either unwilling or unable to see the context of Mary's case, in which a woman was struggling with an alcohol addiction and desperate to find help even if it meant submitting herself to prison. Instead of assistance, he gave her one further month of imprisonment with hard labour. Mary was removed from the court weeping.

Just under ten years after her suicide attempt at the railway station, in 1894, Mary faced her fifty-fourth conviction. She was apprehended by Police Constable Vine for 'being drunk and disorderly and using obscene language'.

Constable Vine brought her to court in the following circumstances, as reported from the court:

> On Friday night he saw the prisoner surrounded by a crowd of boys in the high street, Mitcham. She was shouting and making a great disturbance, and as she was drunk and refused to go away he took her into custody. She refused to walk until the ambulance arrived, and then she danced and shouted all the way to the police station. The prisoner denied being drunk and denounced Vine as a 'false swearing beast of a policeman', adding that she would not care if he spoke the truth ... the prisoner had been fifty-three times previously convicted. The chief clerk said the bench had tried on many occasions to do something for the prisoner's benefit, but she would not stay in a home, and could not control herself. Magistrates needed the power to send such a woman to a home for inebriates. The magistrate dealing with her case on this occasion had not dealt with her, himself, before. Thus instead of following this course of action, he felt obliged to fine her, instead, the total of twenty-one shillings. If she could not pay she would have to undergo fourteen days in prison.

In the next four years Mary was apprehended for drunkenness over forty more times, causing chaos not only in her own life, but for her husband and sons also. It is hard to believe that Mary was just forty-eight years old when she was charged for the ninety-ninth time for being drunk and disorderly in 1899, and just fifty years old when she died the following year, in all likelihood from the effects of decades of alcohol abuse.

Disorder on the streets

Drunkenness was a problem for lawmakers and politicians because of the public spectacle it presented and the immorality it was thought to encourage in the populace. It was considered that indulgence in alcohol caused those who drank to turn to theft in order to fund their habits and, in the case of women, encouraged prostitution as they attempted to support their deviant lifestyles. Drink was felt to erode both men and women's work ethic, their sense of propriety and good Christian family values. Drunkenness was also problematic because it was connected to a range of other offences. A high proportion of damage to property and public obscenity and cases of 'causing a nuisance' were linked to drunkenness and drunken prostitutes. Inebriated women caused scenes in the streets and smashed windows in violent outbursts.

Huddersfield-born Sarah Gillerlane was the daughter of two Irish immigrants who had come to England at the time of the Great Famine. Her father John worked as a mason's labourer to provide for the family but died when Sarah was just fifteen. The Gillerlane family broke apart. The following year, Sarah married Benjamin Brook, a local miner, and the year after that she began receiving convictions for public order offences. From 1868, Sarah began spending from a few days to two months in prison at regular intervals. Most of her convictions were for street-based disorder such as fighting with others, disorderly conduct and obscene language in public. In five years, Sarah gained fifteen convictions: three for assault, two more for fighting, three for using obscene language, four for drunken disorder, two for theft, and one for obstructing a footpath when she was drunk. Sarah was apprehended for several other public order infractions but managed to avoid conviction when the cases came to court. Almost all of her offences, whether formally part of the charge or not, were related to Sarah's alcohol use. Sarah occasionally worked as a prostitute and associated with similar women who when in drink would fight amongst themselves or with others and also present a loud and obnoxious display on the streets. On one appearance in court alongside two fellow prostitutes a judge suggested of Sarah and her friends that 'society would be better without them' before sending them for a punishment of hard labour.

The lack of assistance available to those battling a range of social and personal problems from homelessness to bereavement or breakdown of relationships saw many women turn to alcohol. Likewise, a lack of understanding about how and why people used alcohol and an absence of assistance for those struggling with addiction saw many trapped in an alarming cycle of petty offending, public disorder and persecution for drunkenness that was almost impossible to escape.

A horrible life

Prostitute Ellen Forbes began working the streets of Westminster in 1867 at the age of just seventeen. As far as records show it took a few years for her to come to the attention of police for drunkenness, disorder and solicitation. Then in just a seven-year period from 1871–78, Ellen managed more than a hundred court appearances. During this time, Ellen was apprehended not for serious violence or thefts that ended in notable terms of imprisonment, but for drunkenness, disorder and bad language, which might involve just a few days in the local lockup.

In the 1870s Ellen found herself in a relentless cycle that saw her apprehended on almost every day on which she was not already in police custody. Ellen had spent six of seven years inside of prison. Ellen's offending record suggests that her offences took place approximately once every three days when she was not already under sentence. Hers was a staggering cycle of behaviour that would leave virtually no other time in which to pursue employment or a social and family life.

Ellen's offences were often attributed to one of the most common excuses used by women arrested for drunk and disorderly behaviour. They would argue that, having only just come out of prison, they were quickly overcome by even the smallest amount of alcohol that they imbibed to celebrate release. In 1872, for example, Ellen was released after spending two weeks in prison on a charge of drunk and disorderly behaviour. She was released alongside a 'bad-looking' woman with whom she had made friends while incarcerated. The two women proceeded to get drunk almost immediately. They then went looking for her companion's belongings, which she believed to have been stolen while she was in prison. Within hours, both women were arrested again for causing a disturbance. Ellen and her companion were sent straight back to prison for another seven days of hard labour.

In 1874, Ellen was found to be drunk and disorderly and was charged with trying to assault the police when they tried to take her into custody. She was sentenced to two months of hard labour. When sentence was pronounced, she picked up the nearest inkwell and attempted to throw it at a police constable. When taken to the cells Ellen began 'singing and dancing'. The levity with which Ellen was able to treat appearing in court and a two-month prison sentence illustrates the sad futility of the cycle in which the courts and offenders like Ellen found themselves. Prison had no impact on Ellen's behaviour or likelihood of reoffending because, in reality, life in prison was no more unpleasant or difficult than the life she led as a prostitute at the mercy of London's streets. On Christmas Eve 1877, she had been ordered to spend three months in a prison for being a 'rogue and a vagabond'. One police constable labelled her 'the most incorrigible woman he had ever known'. Ellen, on the other hand, claimed that 'the police were always down on her and would not leave her alone'.

In 1876, Ellen was charged again with drunk and disorderly conduct. She had already spent several terms in prison that year. Ellen was also sent to prison in default of paying a forty-shilling fine. She was arrested in 1878 for being a 'disorderly prostitute'. She was drunk and fighting with another woman. When a police officer tried to move her away, she began using obscene and insulting language and attempted to kick him 'in a delicate part of the person'. With little sympathy, the local magistrate pronounced:

> He was afraid she would end her days in prison. All he could do now with her would be to commit her as an incorrigible rogue, and she would be kept for hard labour until the next sessions, there to be sentenced, and she would probably have a long sentence that would teach her sober habits.

Both the magistrate and Ellen herself must have been aware that her history and her propensity to turn to alcohol on every release from prison meant that the idea that another term of imprisonment would do anything other than result in the same outcome was ridiculous.

Like the scores of other prostitutes in and out of trouble with the law and in the throes of addiction, after she was of no more interest to newspaper journalists, Ellen disappeared from the historical record. Nothing remains to tell us of how life proceeded for her after the age of twenty-eight.

Battling the bobbies

Ideologically the need to clamp down on vice and drunkenness came from the very top of society but practically when it came to policing public order attention was focused not on society as a whole but very definitely on the working classes. Based on ideas that crime, particularly drunkenness and disorder was inherently a working-class problem, poorer areas of towns and cities became an increasing target for law enforcement. Particular groups, such as prostitutes or ex-offenders, might repeatedly find themselves the object of negative police attention as officers attempted to 'clean up' the streets. As a result even relatively innocuous activities in which women were involved, like drinking in public, rowdy gatherings in communal spaces, vagrancy or even street commerce, could see them liable to arrest. Once the police became involved, it was common for such incidents to erupt into violence, especially those that involved drunkenness. Disputes between local women and the police occurred everywhere. Certain locations with areas of acute poverty, with poor employment prospects for women, or large working-class communities that were poorly integrated with their middle-class contemporaries saw problems more frequently than others. Violence against the police was one of the key problems associated with both drunkenness and prostitution.

In November 1886 in Sunderland, Jane Ann Douse was charged with being drunk and disorderly, and for using bad language. As Police Constable Trotter attempted to escort her down the road to the police station she pulled his whistle out of his uniform and broke the chain. She also tore the buttons off his coat, and when he attempted to restrain her, she bit his hand in three places. Jane was given the choice of paying a two-shilling fine or spending seven days in gaol.

Alice Ward of Croydon was charged with the use of obscene language in public and fined. As she heard the sentence in court, Alice became verbally and then physically violent to those in the courtroom. Striking out with arms and legs, she assaulted two policemen. It eventually took five officers and an ambulance to take her back to the police station so that she could be charged again for a new offence.

When Police Constable Dawson attempted to intervene when Eliza Mangham drunkenly assaulted a man in Burnley, she 'kicked him and pulled him down. She then kicked him on the legs several times.' Dawson had to get a fellow officer to help him take her to the police station to be charged. Police Constable Greenwood of Hull met with a similar problem when he tried to arrest Alicia Murray for being disorderly on a bridge. Alicia, who had previous convictions for assault, was sentenced to thirty days in prison for striking and kicking the officer.

In Birkenhead, Margaret Day had only just been released from an eight-year prison sentence when she had 'too much to drink' and was again apprehended for drunk and disorderly behaviour. She was displeased at the officer who had arrested her, vowing, 'I'll do it, and I'll do for him when I come out.' She then threw an object from her pocket at the police constable. She also assaulted the gaol keeper. Margaret was brought back from the cells to face a subsequent assault charge and given a further two months. On hearing the new sentence she 'sprang' at Police Sergeant Johnson, clutched him round the neck, and then got hold of his legs and tried to bring him to the floor. She was removed to the cells and she continued to kick violently at the door until her boots were removed.

At times, attacks on the police by women could be nothing more than a violent outburst of one stranger against another – isolated moments when frustration bubbled over into violence. On other occasions, attacks on the police were perpetrated by women who had several previous convictions and who were well known to the police. Rightly or wrongly, these women perceived themselves to be harassed and victimised by the authorities. When women became recognised by the police as repeat offenders, it became increasingly difficult for them to find work, socialise or even frequent the streets of their neighbourhood without police intervention. Drinking in pubs could become particularly problematic. Such circumstances saw women labelled as habitual offenders and as a result turn increasingly belligerent and violent towards police officers generally or towards particular constables whom they felt would not allow them to make a fresh start.

In North Shields in 1888, 21-year-old Margaret Bainbridge was drunk and disorderly in the Scarborough Bridge Inn when she assaulted the landlord, John Handslip, after he refused to serve her any more alcohol. Margaret became abusive to Handslip as he unsuccessfully attempted to remove her from the premises. A policeman arrived to assist in Margaret's removal and she 'struck and kicked them both and behaved in a most violent manner on the way to the police station.' Margaret faced three separate charges for drunkenness and assault when she appeared in court days later. Unsurprisingly, this was not Margaret's first offence; she had a history of violence, drunkenness and theft that stretched back years. Earlier that year, Margaret had appeared at the same police court charged with being drunk and disorderly in the same area and assaulting a man by the name of Joseph Hutchinson. She was given two fines. It was noted that Margaret was 'a very bad character' and that she had appeared eight times before. The previous year, Margaret had been so drunk and disorderly that it was necessary to convey her to the police station in a wheelbarrow.

Margaret had several other convictions for public order offences such as being unable to account for herself or for items found in her possession, soliciting as a prostitute, and drunkenness. No record exists of Margaret undertaking any paid employment other than prostitution. Her regular convictions for drunkenness and disorder indicate that she led a somewhat disrupted lifestyle. She was known to the police as a notorious character who associated with other prostitutes and thieves. Into her forties, Margaret was still living in South Shields in a house with multiple occupants. Many fellow residents lived lives as disrupted as Margaret's. In 1901, for example, Margaret was a witness in a coroner's inquest when the 60-year-old man who rented lodgings above her was found dead from excessive alcohol consumption. Most of Margaret's offences and her existence in general were compounded by the violence she exhibited towards the policemen who attempted to arrest or question her when she was drunk. Violence against the police not only reflected badly for women like Margaret in court but also earned them the resentment of officers working the local area, and made it increasingly likely such women would be targeted by the police any time they were in public.

Birmingham's brewery blacklist

The police and courts were not alone in their attempts to control the menace of drunkenness that plighted towns and cities across the country. Towards the end of the nineteenth century, pubs and breweries were made increasingly responsible for the alcohol consumed on their premises, as well as for those they served. There had always been fines awaiting those found selling alcohol illegally or using unlicensed premises as beerhouses but as the twentieth century dawned, authorities sought to increase the powers and punishments they extended over the legal pubs and publicans that supplied alcohol to some of England's most troublesome characters.

The *Holt Brewery Black List* is an example of one such method used in Birmingham. The book provided a list of men and women designated as habitual drunkards. The 1902 amendment to the Licensing Act made it an offence for those identified as 'habitual drunkards' (those with three or more convictions for drunkenness or related offences) to attempt to purchase or consume intoxicating liquids. At the same time, this legislation left licensed premises and individuals liable to prosecution if they served alcohol to those in breach of the act. Documents like the *Holt Brewery's Black List* were created by committee with the help of local authorities to assist publicans and licensed individuals identify and refuse service to local habitual drunkards. The blacklist was intended to help both publicans and authorities. In theory, the courts restricted the availability of alcohol to some of the most notorious problem drinkers in the district, the police had fewer cases of drunk and disorderly behaviour to attend to, which saved time, money and considerable aggravation, and publicans would be rid of some of their most problematic and destructive customers. No conclusive proof exists as to the effectiveness of such schemes. It seems doubtful that alcohol-related offences were stopped by this measure. It is more likely that men and women placed on a blacklist simply found other ways to come by alcohol, or moved to other locations where their identities were not known. In this sense, the problem shifted from place to place rather than reduced. There are also accounts of individuals becoming belligerent or abusive towards publicans who refused to serve them and damage done to property when they were asked to leave.

The 1903–1904 blacklist contained pages for eighty-three individuals convicted of drunk and disorderly offences. Thirty-seven of those included were women. Typically, by the time women were placed on the habitual drunkards register they were in their mid-thirties to mid-forties and usually had years, if not decades, of convictions and disorder behind them. The information contained within documents like the blacklist allows a small insight into the kinds of women that found themselves labelled as habitual drunks in the era.

Firstly, despite prominent Victorian perceptions, the women did more than drink. All but two of the women were listed as having some kind of employment. Of course this did not mean that they were currently employed at the time of their addition to the register, only that they identified themselves, or were identified by the police, with a particular occupation or set of skills. Most of Birmingham's female habitual drunks were manual labourers and street workers. They staffed the factories that had seen the city become one of England's industrial hubs. They worked as metal polishers, press operators and machine hands. Factory work was hard, with long hours, dangerous conditions and poor pay. Demand for such work always outstripped the number of jobs available and as a result job security for female workers was poor. Even more common than factory work amongst the women on the blacklist was street work. Female drunks made a living as hawkers (street sellers) or charwomen (cleaners), whilst others sought work house to house doing laundry or sewing. Unsurprisingly, a number of the women also worked as prostitutes. They may not have obtained their sole living through prostitution but relied upon the trade as a strategy to cope with times of financial hardship to supplement their earnings, or in order to make money for extras such as alcohol, entertainment or clothing.

The descriptions given on the blacklist tell us not only what the women did for a living and their names, ages and aliases, but also physical and residential descriptions, which give an indication of the difficult and unpleasant circumstances of many women battling with alcohol dependency in the period. About a quarter of the women had no listed place of abode. The rest inhabited either slum-like court dwellings or temporary accommodation. Only a few of the women were married; most had an unstable or poorly developed family support network leaving them largely alone to deal with their addictions and convictions. The life of a habitual drunkard was a lonely one with few securities and comforts. It could be a dangerous one, too. Virtually all of the women convicted of drunkenness and placed on the blacklist had scars or disfigurements. These could range from the relatively commonplace like scalds and missing teeth to the serious, in which there were knife wounds or even missing fingers or eyes. In general, the women had mild facial scarring such as cut marks on the forehead or cheeks, and several had scars and the signs of broken noses. Facial scaring and scars to the arms and legs were products of fighting and attacks that would have been familiar to those who spent time in the rough communities of Victorian England.

Alice Loxley was a typical example of one of the women on Birmingham's habitual drunkards register. When Alice was placed on the blacklist in 1903 at the age of thirty-four, she already had a history of drunkenness that dated back more than a decade. Alice worked as a hawker. Her face bore the marks and scars of numerous fights and her arms the tattooed initials of significant loved ones and former lovers. In 1892, Alice was involved in an argument with another woman by the name of Margaret Finn in the notorious White Lion Yard pub in Birmingham. The two women drunkenly quarrelled quite incredibly over a theft that had occurred more than fourteen years previously. As the heat of the dispute rose, Margaret pulled a knife and stabbed Alice in the head. In 1894, Alice was charged with drunkenly damaging property and assaulting two police officers who had arrived to stop her. Concerned neighbours had summoned the police after they heard Alice 'smashing up the furniture' in the room she lodged in. When the constables arrived, Alice wildly swung around the broken leg of a table, singing, 'Well keep it up: my birthday comes but once a year. Let's keep it up, let's keep it up'. When Alice appeared in court a few days later she was a well-recognised figure, it being noted that she had several previous convictions. Alice was nonplussed when taken from the dock, sentenced to two months' imprisonment, and began singing. Alice was seemingly unfazed by a custodial sentence, indicating that she was no stranger to the proceedings and that perhaps her existence outside of prison was not one she was desperate to be left to.

Similarly, Ann Moran's conviction for drunkenness in 1903 masked a tragic tale of a woman living on the edge of endurance. Like so many others on the brewery's blacklist, Ann had seen more than her share of convictions for drunkenness and disorderly conduct. In 1887, Ann was found guilty of smashing every pane of glass in the font windows of her neighbour's house when in a drunken rage. In 1892, Ann and her husband were both prosecuted for drunkenness after police had needed to carry her home, insensible, from a local pub. Ann had been a victim of violence as well as a perpetrator. Ann was stabbed by a man named Robert Bennett, in 1893 (again in the fateful White Lion Yard pub). Ann had been drunkenly quarrelling with Bennett's sister, exchanging blows and pulling hair in a struggle for some time when the other woman called her brother for help. Robert Bennett wasted no time in stabbing Ann twice in the head.

In February 1900, Ann, described by the papers as 'a miserably dressed woman', was prosecuted for 'exposing her children to the elements'. It was reported that when not sleeping rough on the streets, Ann lived in a scarcely habitable building that had been condemned by city officials. Prior to its scheduled demolition, the house had all of the doors and windows removed and was little more than a shell of a dwelling. By squatting with her family in these conditions, Ann was responsible for exposing her children to the weather 'in such a manner as to injure their health'. For six months, Ann had kept her children with her on 'bitterly cold nights' rather than submitting herself to the workhouse or placing her children in institutions. On one occasion, Ann's youngest child was found lying on a doorstep barely clothed in the middle of November while Ann was inside, drunk. The prosecution against her was one of those bought by the relatively newly formed NSPCC. It may have been nothing but negligence or judgement impaired by drunkenness that led Ann to keep her children living in uninhabitable housing through the bitterest months of the year. Certainly, her 'disreputable character' was used in the case against her. Alternatively, Ann's history of convictions and poor relationship with the authorities may have dissuaded her from seeking help from institutions such as the workhouse in a time of need. The perception of Ann's immoral character may have disqualified her from many forms of relief anyway. What's more, Ann may have been unwilling to give up her children to an organisation that would care for them knowing that once surrendered, it would be very difficult for a destitute woman and habitual drunk living in a derelict building to regain custody.

After her conviction Ann was sent to prison for two months of hard labour and both of her children were placed in the Middlemore Children's Emigration Home. In this home orphaned, abandoned or neglected children like Ann's were housed prior to transportation to Canada. The children were sent abroad for adoption without the consent of their parents so that they might start a new life far away from the circumstances and abject poverty of their beginnings. The year after Ann's imprisonment only one of her children remained in the home. The other child had very possibly been sent to Canada. Ann was imprisoned again the following year, and the next trace of her after that was the conviction for drunk and disorderly at the beginning of 1903 that landed her on the brewery's blacklist. It is not possible to trace Ann after this time. Those with no fixed address often slip through the cracks of formal record keeping like the census. Having lost her children and undergone a citywide ban from drinking establishments Ann may have moved on to begin again. She may have stayed in Birmingham, sleeping on the streets or in abandoned buildings, continuing the cycle of petty offences too routine to be of interest to even the local police court column in the newspaper.

The information available on Ann Moran's life shows both the cause and effect nature of drunkenness in the declining quality of life of many 'habitual' drunkards around the country. For women enduring a daily grind of financial insecurity and a struggle to subsist, alcohol might offer a cheap route of socialising with others in the same position, entertainment or escape – even if just for a matter of hours. However, the public-order offences that so often arose with the use of alcohol, such as violence, damage to property or disorderly behaviour, only served to create more problems from which women sought to escape. Alcohol addiction reduced opportunities to earn a living, ate away at already meagre funds and, just as in Ann's case, could cost women their homes, families and liberty. A lack of social understanding and support meant that with each loss or difficulty women experienced because of their use of alcohol, the more their lives descended into chaos and the less they had anything other than alcohol to turn to. The cycle of alcohol abuse and conviction could establish itself so overwhelmingly that women felt powerless to stop it.

'One of the worst characters in Birmingham'

Alice Maud Tatlow's life began in India in 1878, where her father, John, was a sergeant in the 109th Foot Regiment of the British Army. John and his wife Mary Ann had been married in Birmingham in 1868 and were both previously from 'traveller' families. The following year, John, who worked primarily as a gunsmith, had joined the army and been deployed to India. It was there that the Tatlows lived for almost a decade and had five children, of whom Alice was the second to last. The family returned to England in 1880, when Alice was three years old. The Tatlows moved first to the garrison town of Aldershot in Hampshire, where John was demobilised, before they settled permanently back in Birmingham.

There is little information about Alice's early life or when or why her problematic drinking first began. In 1900, Alice was convicted of fraud. She had on several occasions that year applied to a charitable fund run by the *Birmingham Daily Mail* for the relief of servicemen's families. Alice had claimed that her father was fighting in the Boer War in South Africa and that she needed funds to buy a respectable outfit so that she might get a domestic service position. It is unknown what Alice spent the money on (possibly alcohol) but it was known that her father was no longer a soldier and that she had no intentions of working in service. This was just the beginning of two decades of well-documented drinking and petty offending for Alice.

Less than four years later, in 1904, Alice was convicted at the Birmingham City Police Court as drunk and disorderly. She was included in the blacklist register and identified as a habitual drunkard. As with all the others on the list, Alice was barred from entering pubs in Birmingham, presumably even the one run by her sister. If the police were to find Alice drinking in a pub, she faced prosecution and the proprietor would be fined. Alice was twenty-five when she appeared on the blacklist, but the information provided about her indicates that she had been living on the margins of respectable society for some time and already had several convictions for drunkenness. It was noted that Alice operated as a prostitute, and had tattoos indicating several criminal associations and the initials of various lovers.

After being placed on the blacklist Alice's life continued to be troubled. By 1911, she had received many more convictions for drunkenness and, like many of Birmingham's habitual drunks, was admitted to the Brentry Certified Inebriate Reformatory, near Bristol. The institution would take both voluntary admissions and those that were court ordered. Magistrates would sentence women who they had convicted a number of times for drunk and disorderly behaviour to be treated at the reformatory for a period of three years. A report on the Brentry Inebriate Reformatory stated:

> The history of such a patient is usually one of poverty, neglected childhood, scanty education and want of proper training and discipline in youth. ... Many give a history of having been brought up 'on the streets', 'canals', 'gipsy encampments' and such like places: in some cases running away from their homes at an early age and commencing a criminal career before they reached their majority.

At places like the Brentry Reformatory sobriety was enforced and medication administered to treat the effects of inebriety. Inmates were 'taught' the value of hard work and clean living. Supervision of patients continued for a year after their discharge.

After release, Alice did not stay sober but instead returned to regular bouts of drunkenness and public order offending. Alice's inability or unwillingness to reform once released from the reformatory was symptomatic not, as contemporaries would have asserted, due to moral weakness or bad character but instead of a life in which difficulty and danger could be unrelenting. Many habitual drunks like Alice were not just the perpetrators of nuisance crimes, violence and thefts, but very often victims as well. Reliance on alcohol was often a coping mechanism for those who found very little support or solace elsewhere. In 1914, Alice took a man named Andrew Franklin to court for assault and theft. Alice claimed that she had met Franklin one night at his request, and after ascertaining how much money Alice had on her, Franklin had struck her down and kicked her in the face before making away with her satchel. Franklin protested his innocence, and his sister testified that Alice herself had absent-mindedly left the satchel of money in Franklin's house. Franklin contended that Alice's injuries had been sustained during a struggle over his hat, which she was trying to steal from him. Franklin was found not guilty.

Whilst the newspaper report is ambiguous about the nature of their meeting, Alice had in all likelihood met Franklin as a prostitute hoping for trade. Sadly, it was not uncommon for prostitutes like Alice to meet with violence from customers. Prostitutes made easy targets for theft as at the end of a shift working the streets and lodging houses they could have cash to the value of several shillings on them. It was not difficult for would-be thieves to lure prostitutes out of public sight to conduct a robbery. As a prostitute and a woman known to the courts as a drunk, a troublemaker, and a thief, it is also unlikely that Alice would have found a sympathetic ally in the police. Alice was notorious as 'one of the worst characters in Birmingham' and so it is largely unsurprising that her pursuit of justice was unsuccessful. The court was not predisposed to be in her favour, and with few witnesses and no evidence, the value of her world was not enough for a jury.

Ultimately, institutions like the Inebriate's Reformatory or short spells of imprisonment did little to address the root causes of drunkenness or offer help to those living in the chaotic grip of addiction. Most of the mechanisms used to deal with women like Alice were punitive rather than rehabilitative and unfortunately this resulted all too often in an inability to desist from damaging and disorderly lifestyles. In April 1914, Alice attempted suicide. She was drunk at the time, following, she claimed, the funeral of her brother. A detective from the Midland Railway company told that shortly after midnight on the day in question he saw Alice deliberately jump in front of a train. Several bystanders jumped down onto the tracks to rescue her. Had the stationary train moved a yard further, Alice would have been killed instantly. When asked why she had put herself in such danger a drunken Alice exclaimed, 'I want to die. I have buried my brother and I don't want to live any longer.' Alice remained unrepentant for the act and when taken to the police station to face charges she stated, 'Why did you not let me die?'

In 1915, Alice was apprehended for breaking a window, the property of her neighbour, a man by the name of Joseph Bleser. Alice had been drunk one Friday evening and was witnessed by a police officer throwing an object through the window. Alice reportedly disliked Bleser because he was a German. As she broke the window Alice was heard to shout, 'When the *Lusitania* went down he went to hoist a flag. He is a German; that is what he is.' Bleser was proved to be a patriot of Britain who had done much to assist the war refugees from Belgium living in Birmingham. Alice was sent to prison for two months. In 1917, Alice was sent to prison for a month after using obscene language one night in the street. One month would seem an excessively heavy punishment for this offence, but Alice's reputation no doubt made magistrates keen to remove her from the streets of the city for as long as possible. At the beginning of 1918, Alice was again in court. She was convicted of stealing a purse containing a few shillings from a local barmaid. Alice had robbed the barmaid while she was serving in the pub where Alice was drinking. When apprehended a little while later by the barmaid who noticed her purse was missing, Alice claimed that she had only taken the purse for a 'swank' to show off. Alice was sent to prison for twelve months of hard labour.

By 1918, Alice was forty years old and had been convicted of more than eighty offences. Institutional and conviction records are closed to the public for 100 years and so we know very little about Alice after the end of the First World War. Alice remained living in Birmingham for the remainder of her life. At different times, Alice made a living as a bookie's runner, by taking in sewing and, of course, prostitution. She never married or had children of her own, but remained in touch with her siblings and their children and grandchildren. She was a well-known and easily recognised figure in her local area. Despite continuing to drink long into her later life, Alice lived until 1960, dying at the quite remarkable age of eighty-two (see plate 18).

Birmingham is just one location in which drunkenness was prevalent and official responses to it were inadequate, both in terms of providing a solution to the problems caused by alcohol and in offering real and lasting assistance to the women who lost their lives to drink. One of the most striking things about female drunkenness in Victorian England was just how closely it was linked to prostitution. Drunken disorder was just one of the common problems caused by women caught up in the 'great social evil' of the era.

The great social evil

The common prostitute is one of the most well known of Victorian wayward women. The 'lady of the night', 'fallen woman', 'street walker' or simply 'unfortunate' has graced the pages of novels and appeared on theatre stages and television screens in the years that have passed since she was first noticed turning her trade in the streets of England. Prostitutes have been the stuff of bawdy music hall ballads and Dickensian tragedy alike. The prostitute herself is instantly recognisable in depictions past and present by her painted face and gaudy clothes, her loud mouth and heart of gold. This description of Nancy and Bet from *Oliver Twist*, two of the most famous fictional prostitutes of the era, is just one example:

> They wore a good deal of hair, not very neatly turned up behind and rather untidy about the shoes and stockings. They were not exactly pretty, perhaps; but they had a great deal of colour in their faces, and looked quite stout and hearty being remarkably free and agreeable in their manners.

Like so many other types of female offending, the reality of prostitution in England was far less bright and cheerful than the fine life certain fictional works have presented to us. The world of Victorian prostitution was a dark one. The women who sold their bodies for a fee often lived lives of acute poverty and violence. They faced danger at the hands of their clients, those that managed them, the police and even each other. Prostitutes presented a challenge to Victorian moral sensibilities because they not only flouted the sexual norms of the time but also because the world of the sex trade was one in which other kinds of crime and vice were allowed to flourish.

It has never been precisely clear how many women worked as prostitutes in this period, who they worked for or who exactly was their customer base. William Acton, one of the foremost writers on prostitution and its evils in Victorian England, was as much at a loss as we are now to providing accurate figures for the extent of prostitution in England. After collecting information from magistrates, religious officials and charities he estimated that at the beginning of the Victorian period in London alone there were anywhere from 50,000 to 80,000 women working as prostitutes. Only a fraction of this number came into contact with the police and courts. In each large town and city across the country just a few thousand prostitutes were prosecuted every year whilst many times more plied their trade anonymously. (See plate 19.)

Sex work was, and remains, difficult to trace for a number of reasons. Apart from exceptional examples, prostitution as a trade in the Victorian era left very little paper record. There were no employment documents or transaction receipts. Unless apprehended by the police as they worked, it is difficult to know if all women labelled as prostitutes actually were sex workers. Some women were falsely accused or even convicted of prostitution and other women who worked as prostitutes were never found or identified as such. Prostitution was not always a full-time or permanent occupation for those women involved. Some women may have resorted to exchanging sex for money only occasionally or in isolated periods of need, so may not have considered themselves prostitutes in the real sense.

When considering the activities of Victorian prostitutes it is vital to remember that what we discover of the trade and the women involved in it might only partially apply to some, not hold true for others and be applicable to a range of women that we will never be able to identify. However, whilst this uncertainty stands, the Victorian fascination with vice has left behind sufficient documentation for us to explore the world of Victorian prostitution and the varied roles women played within it, from walking the streets to running the trade.

Prostitution and prostitutes

The first and most important distinction to be made about prostitution in the Victorian era is that it was not actually a criminal offence. Nonetheless, women who worked as prostitutes constituted the largest single group of female offenders arrested and prosecuted in the courts over the course of the nineteenth century. Attitudes towards women more generally in the period meant that the prostitute came to symbolise the very opposite of proper and respectable femininity. Quite simply, the prostitute was the Victorian anti-woman. Where a woman's proper place was considered to be in the home, she could also be found in the streets. If a woman was expected to be quiet and demure, the prostitute was brash and unashamed. Decency demanded chastity and purity from a woman but the prostitute sold her body to the highest bidder. From a social, moral and cultural perspective, even if not from a legal one, the prostitute was perceived by many as a scourge of the decent world.

Much of the Victorian period was given over to debates about how best prostitution might be contained or stopped and how prostitutes might be dealt with. A range of loosely worded legislation allowed for the prosecution of prostitutes. The woman who touted for business openly in public could be apprehended for soliciting. If prostitutes were soliciting in busy public streets, they might also find themselves charged with obstructing a public thoroughfare. Those who refused to be moved on, or made too much of a show of themselves, could be arrested for causing a public nuisance or for disorderly conduct. Certainly, as we have seen, evidence is plentiful that there was no love lost between beat constables and the women who worked on England's streets.

However, it would be remiss to present the trouble that often happened to women working as prostitutes as solely a product of police oppression. The social and spatial worlds of these women allowed behaviours that challenged law and order to flourish. Prostitutes were regularly found in breach of public order regulations and exhibiting episodes of interpersonal violence. The cases of drunkenness already mentioned are just some of the many examples that show the destructive and anti-social behaviour that prostitutes, particularly when inebriated, were responsible for.

Jane Butt, a local of Warwickshire, received her first conviction 1872, when she was thirty-six. Jane had been working the streets of Aston as a prostitute for an unknown period of time before she came to the attention of the courts for public drunkenness. In the following year, she had two more convictions for drunkenness. In 1874, she held four convictions for drunkenness and riotous behaviour. In 1875 and 1876, she was again arrested for drunkenness, and in 1877 she began to be formally recognised and charged as a 'disorderly prostitute'. In all likelihood, this meant that she was found carrying out the same behaviours as she had in previous years but by this time, the police had apprehended her as she was also working the streets. That same year, Jane had two more convictions just for drunkenness. As time progressed Jane was clearly spending an increasing amount of time plying her trade as a prostitute, or perhaps just becoming more readily identifiable to local police constables, as she began to be arrested not only for drunkenness and disorder but also simply for the very poorly defined crime of 'street walking'.

By the end of 1879, Jane had been convicted of public order offences relating to prostitution eighteen times. She may well have been arrested much more often than her convictions indicate. Convictions for drunkenness saw her receive sentences of from seven to fourteen days of hard labour, and offences where she was formally charged as a prostitute earned her one month with hard labour. There is evidence to suggest that prior to her arrests, and even during her public order infractions of the 1870s, Jane also worked as a dressmaker whenever she could in order to support herself. Prostitution may have initially been an employment that she turned to in order to supplement poor wages or when she suffered a downturn in business or a personal crisis. Yet this tactic proved for Jane, and many others, to be a double-edged sword. Although prostitution may have produced extra funds to alleviate financial problems in the short term the frequent prosecutions that saw Jane regularly spend from a week to a month in prison would have severely affected her ability to find or complete any other kind of paying work. The social stigma and wider repercussions that could face women who worked the streets as prostitutes would also damage their prospects for employment and social stability. Thus, Jane found herself in a vicious circle of behaviour in which the more she worked as a prostitute to supplement lost earnings the harder it became for her to earn money in any other way.

Many explanations for why women like Jane turned to prostitution throughout the nineteenth century presented women who worked as prostitutes as physically, mentally and morally defective. The first and most overwhelming consensus about prostitutes is that they were sexually deviant women who had given themselves over to their craven and 'uncontrollable sexual desires'. Women who flaunted their sexuality and succumbed to sexual activity outside of marriage were considered already on the path to professional vice. William Acton even went as far as to suggest that all of the thousands of unwed mothers in England had 'taken the first step in prostitution' by being so careless with their virtue. Other than sexual depravity, those engaged in prostitution were accused of vanity, profligacy and a 'love of dress', which overrode proper social and moral values.

Occasionally prostitution was explained by unfortunate circumstances, a poor start in life or an unexpected crisis that saw women sink to the lowest depths in order to survive. However, for every prostitute who elicited sympathy many more were considered lazy and indolent. Idle women, it was suggested, wanted to work as prostitutes because it was an easy option that offered less arduous work than that available in factories or domestic jobs. Yet the accounts we have of women in Victorian England suggest that for the overwhelming majority of individuals, working as a prostitute was a brutal and brutalising existence.

In April 1880, Jane Butt was still working as a prostitute in her local area of Aston (see plates 20 and 21). One of her neighbours, Ada Jarvis, ran an 'improper house' – a location where drink could be purchased, gambling could take place and prostitutes could work. When Jane confronted Ada and accused her of doing such, Ada denied it. Enraged at either Ada's denial or refusal to admit her to the house where there were potential customers, Jane struck Ada in the face and then pulled a knife and stabbed her in the forehead and shoulder. Ada was seriously injured and had to be attended by a surgeon. Jane was quickly arrested for the crime and sent to trial, where she received a five-year prison sentence.

During her time as a prostitute, Jane had become estranged from her family. Although she was recorded as being married and having one child her husband did not contact her for the duration of her time in prison. Jane had evidently not seen other members of her family for some time, even though they also lived in Warwickshire. In 1881, Mrs Osborne, identified as Jane's sister, wrote a pleading letter to the superintendent of the prison in which Jane was serving her sentence. The local police could not give any information on Jane, and Osborne wrote to the superintendent: 'On the subject of Jane Butt, is she alive or not?'

Jane was initially released on licence in 1883, but very quickly returned to prostitution. She was arrested in 1884 for soliciting and returned to prison to serve one month for the offence, and the rest of the sentence of her previous conviction. She was released again in 1885. After spending such a long time in prison and realising that any law breaking was likely to end in immediate rearrest, Jane went to stay with her sister. Months later, a police report found her to finally be 'well conducted'. After this time, all records for Jane disappear. She might have stayed with her sister and built a life that did not involve prostitution. She may have chosen to move away and leave her troubled past behind her. She may have stayed in Warwickshire, taking on a new identity or reverting to an old one. Jane Butt was never served another sentence of penal servitude. Her time in London's convict prisons may have been what was required to help her reform her life. Under a different name or in another location she may well have continued to work as a prostitute, or breach public order with drunkenness or disorderly behaviour. Evidence as to whether women like Jane managed to escape their troubled past seldom remains.

For all its problems, prostitution was a sometimes solution to financial hardship. Some forms of prostitution could certainly be more profitable than the other employments open to working-class women. What a factory girl or street seller might earn in a week, a prostitute could earn in a day. Prostitution was perhaps a form of economic individualism for some women. Prostitutes were, in some cases, more finely dressed than their wage-earning counterparts were. They might have more time and disposable income, too. Money was not the only factor though. For every woman that sought a life of full-time prostitution instead of domestic or factory work, there were scores more that took to prostitution as a last resort when other means of self-sufficiency had failed. Many prostitutes were women pushed into the profession by an unscrupulous agent, or those who used prostitution to fund lives of addiction or the needs of others. Along with the money earned through prostitution itself, women took what profits they could from stealing and trading in the goods of their hapless customers.

Rose Callaghan was born in Ireland and moved to Preston, Lancashire, as a young child. She grew up with her parents and sisters only a stone's throw from the notorious brothels and drinking houses close to Preston's railway station. Given the nature of her early environment, perhaps it is little surprise that she spent most of her adult life working as a prostitute in Preston. Rose touted the streets and pubs for custom of her own and was, from time to time, the proprietor of a house that she used as a brothel. When running a brothel Rose took her own customers and allowed other prostitutes, including her younger sister Elizabeth, to operate there for a share of their earnings. The evidence we can gather of Rose's life allows insight into the daily interactions experienced by prostitutes in her position. Rose's life was one of poverty and violence in a largely hidden world in which the community governed itself. Whilst the police and town authorities did not promote the trade in vice in any certain areas, they felt if they allowed it to remain uninhibited at particular locations it could be contained and kept a safe distance from polite society. Those foolish enough to enter a notorious hotspot of prostitution, gambling and disorderly houses did so at their own risk.

The area in Preston where Rose worked was one such place. In the almost unbelievably named Old Cock Yard there was an 'infamous nest of brothels' in which prostitutes not only traded with relative ease, but also took full advantage of any opportunity to make money from their customers. Rose Callaghan's particular speciality was to rob customers of money, jewellery and even clothing either while they were insensible through drink or with the use of violence. She did not act alone. Usually she conspired with other prostitutes, friends, family and the proprietors of the brothels in which she was working in order to carry out her offences.

At the beginning of 1878, Rose and a fellow woman of 'easy virtue', Elizabeth Haighton, were charged with stealing £12 from farmer William Rawcliffe. The prosecution asserted that when in Preston a couple of weeks previously Rawcliffe had passed Rose and Elizabeth at the door to their lodgings, a brothel. The two women had enquired if he wanted to come inside for a drink. Shortly after entering, Elizabeth restrained Rawcliffe's arms while Rose rifled through his waistcoat and trousers, taking the money. Rawcliffe was then 'bundled' out of the house. He went immediately to find a constable and took him to identify the women. In court, it transpired that Rawcliffe was no stranger to Rose and Elizabeth. It was in fact the second time he had been robbed by them. Rawcliffe maintained that he had only ended up by their lodgings by accident but it is more than likely that knowing them to be prostitutes he had approached their lodgings with the purpose of procuring their services.

Along with two friends in September 1881, Rose robbed a man named Michael Smith of belongings with an estimated value of £6. Smith had been out drinking with Rose and her friends and was later enticed back to Rose's house, where he claimed to have fallen asleep in a chair. While he was asleep, the three women rifled through his pockets, taking anything of value before disappearing. In April 1882, Rose and a fellow prostitute were convicted of robbing Benjamin Beaumont of his watch, chain and guard, valued at £5. Beaumont had, he contended, been in a local pub where he met with Rose and her friend Harriet before accompanying them to a brothel. Once inside with the door closed, Preston police court heard how the women 'set upon him, kicked him on the face so as to disfigure him, and robbed him of his watch and guard.' Rose and Harriet then made good their escape while Beaumont recovered. Beaumont saw Rose later and attempted to follow her home but as he reached the yard he was struck down by a man (a friend, partner or even pimp who worked with her). Unfortunately for Rose, all of the commotion brought the attention of the police and she and Harriet were found and arrested. Rather surprisingly, when the case came to court they were both acquitted. It was suggested by the prosecution in a later case against Rose that she, and many like her, often avoided prosecution for offences such as these because jurors were loath find a case in favour of a man that they perceived as immoral for having dealings with prostitutes. Rose Callaghan was said to have unusual good luck in this regard. (See plate 22.)

We only know of a minority of cases like Rose's because successful prosecutions were rare. Men who consorted with prostitutes were not likely to find particular sympathy in court. Other victims never reported their ordeals because of a reluctance to admit in public, to employers or to their families that they had been in the company of prostitutes. Rose Callaghan was prosecuted for this kind of offence on a regular basis. In all probability, she committed far more than were ever brought to the attention of the police. The year after Rose robbed Beaumont her luck ran out. In 1883, along with two other prostitutes she was convicted for another formulaic robbery in which she stole £16 from a customer named Frank Conner. Conner, a member of the army reserve, had drawn several months' pay before heading into Preston to spend it. He met Rose and her associates in a pub and at her insistence followed them back to a house. Once there Connor was given something to drink and was immediately rendered 'insensible'. When he came to he was outside the house and all of his money was gone. In the meantime, Rose and her friends had been on a spending spree. They purchased several articles and paid for them, quite indiscreetly, with Conner's gold. Rose was identified as the ringleader of the operation and all three women were sentenced to five years' imprisonment. As a notably bad character who had been lucky to escape many previous convictions, Rose also had to undergo seven years of police supervision upon release from prison.

The strategy of prostitutes in taking victims back to their lodgings or brothels seems surprising as it made them easily identifiable should victims seek out the assistance of the police. Yet offences of this type were common across England. The stories reported in newspapers will often refer to robbed men as having 'kept company' or 'gone drinking' with prostitutes without elaborating on the true nature of these encounters. Details of such cases were left intentionally vague. There should be no mistake that in a large proportion of the cases the victims were actually customers of women who worked as prostitutes and they had actively sought out the company of these women or returned to their lodgings to exchange money for sex. Once a customer was undressed or asleep, women – either alone or with help –

would rob the unsuspecting man, making off with money, watches and other valuables. At times men awoke to find themselves missing even their boots, shirts and trousers.

Offences of this nature were particularly common in locations in which soldiers and sailors frequented, such as Bristol and Liverpool. Sailors, especially after returning from long periods of time at sea, would receive several months' worth of pay, which they would carry with them while out drinking and paying for the services of prostitutes. Drunken sailors with full pockets were easy pickings for prostitutes, and their clothing and valuables could be quickly pawned. Often these men would only remain in a town or city for a short while before returning to sea, meaning that they did not always have the opportunity to pursue a prosecution. Those who robbed from soldiers in this way were so well known that they were referred to not just as thieves but as 'land sharks'. The small area in which Rose Callaghan lived and worked was known to be a resort of soldiers and sailors and these men were notable amongst her many victims.

Several folk songs originating from the nineteenth century offer cautionary tales of this practice. One of the most famous of these songs originates from Liverpool and lists several of the streets around the notorious centre of prostitution near Lime Street Station. So culturally ingrained was this experience that the song *Maggie May* maintained popularity throughout the twentieth century and into the twenty-first. One version of the highly variable lyrics is as follows:

> *Oh come along all you sailor boys and listen to my plea and when*
> *I am finished you'll agree*
> *I was a goddamned fool in the port of Liverpool.*
> *The first time that I came home from sea*
> *We was paid off at The Hove from a port called Sydney Cove*
> *And two pound ten a month was all my pay.*
> *Oh I started drinking gin and was neatly taken in*
> *By a little girl they all called Maggie May.*
>
> Chorus: *Oh Maggie Maggie May, they've taken her away,*
> *And she'll never walk down Lime Street anymore.*

For she's robbed so many sailors and captains of the whalers
That dirty, robbing, no good Maggie May.

'Twas a damned unlucky day when I first met Maggie May,
She was cruising up and down old Canning Place.
Oh she had a figure fine as a warship of the line
And me being a sailor I gave chase.
In the morning when I woke stiff and sore and stoney broke,
No trousers, coat or waistcoat could I find.
The landlady said, 'Sir, I can tell you where they are,
They'll be down in Kelly's nock-shop number nine.'

Another notable sailor song from around the same period titled *Go to Sea no More* notes:

When I returned to Liverpool I went upon the spree
With the money to last I spent it fast,
Got drunk as drunk could be.
Before the money was all spent on liquor and the whores
I made up my mind that I was inclined to go to sea no more.

As I was walking down the street I met with Angeline,
She said, 'Come home with me, me boy, we'll have a cracking time.'
But when I awoke it was no joke, for I found I was all alone,
Me hat, me boots, and me money too,
Me whole ruddy gear was gone.

Despite the money that could be made, the life of the Victorian street prostitute was a hard one. Far from their lifestyle providing financial security prostitutes were often some of the poorest and most desperate women to fill police cells. Many resided in a network of casual lodging houses or faced nights sleeping rough after spending all day out on the streets. Women who worked as prostitutes could struggle with alcohol addiction and their lives were often blighted by complicated relationships, violence and uncertainty.

As well as theft, violence also played a part in Rose Callaghan's everyday life. The violent offences that she committed were very similar to those committed by most prostitutes: brawls or trading insults with other women competing for work and violent outbursts when she came into contact with the police. In 1875, Rose was convicted of assaulting a police officer after two officers entered her house in search of a sailor they were looking for. Rose was sentenced to one month in prison for throwing a lump of coal at one of the constables. In 1883, Rose spent two months in prison for assault, and in 1895, she was summoned to court after blacking the eyes of a Mary Ann Jenkinson. Cases such as the latter were more of a nuisance than a priority for the courts, and on this occasion the case was dismissed with Rose's promise that she would get off the streets and enter the workhouse.

As with cases of theft, not all violence between and against prostitutes was reported. Often the women involved were more concerned with keeping out of court than seeking legal retribution. People who lived on the fringes of the law, such as prostitutes – and brothel keepers, had their own ways of settling disputes and seeking justice. In 1882, Rose was due to appear in court as a witness to a charge of wounding between two local women. Knowing better than to testify against others in her community, Rose absconded, and stayed in hiding for weeks until the case passed. The same case was delayed again when the victim went missing before she could testify. Two years previously, Rose had also refused to testify on her own behalf. Rose was assaulted by Leo Parkinson, the brother of the man she lived with. Rose and Parkinson had both been drinking when Parkinson kicked her 'in the bowels'. Rose did not bring the charge against Parkinson herself; the event was actually witnessed by a policeman who brought Parkinson to court. Rose denied any knowledge of the event and so the case was dismissed.

Rose was not one of the prostitutes and brothel keepers who lived independently on the proceeds of her business. For at least twenty years, Rose's earnings and her working life were controlled by the man with whom she cohabited. William Parkinson was known to the police to be a 'dissolute man' with a long criminal record of his own. William had been convicted of counts of animal cruelly, and the illegal ownership of dogs without a licence. He ran cockfights and dogfights in Preston. When Rose was undergoing her sentence of five years' imprisonment William entered the workhouse, where he proceeded to steal items of clothing. In the same year he was also found guilty of stealing from a prostitute – a former associate of Rose's, Elizabeth Haighton. William had multiple convictions for other thefts and assaults.

In 1882, a case was brought against William for brutally assaulting Rose. She was unable to appear in court due to hospitalisation resulting from the severe violence used against her. Rose had a wound, possibly caused by a knife, which started above her right eye exposing 2 inches of bone, and continued to her upper lip and down to her left breast. She had suffered severe blood loss and also had another wound from a kick on her leg. Rose carried the scars of this attack for the rest of her life. Over ten years later, the pair were still cohabiting and Rose was still working as a prostitute in order to support William. It seems that for almost twenty years, William was not just a common-law husband to Rose but also her pimp. The magistrate who tried the case recounted with distaste that William had for years lived off the proceeds of Rose's prostitution. In August 1895, William returned home to their lodgings drunk and demanded money from Rose. She had earned none that day and had nothing to give him. After a brief argument, a newspaper reported, William 'kicked her black and blue all over. Then he dragged her about by the hair of the head. He had no mercy.' A 'running kick to the forehead' and another 'shameful thrashing' were given to Rose the following day in an assault that used 'very great violence'. Neighbours testified to having heard screams and cries of 'Murder!' coming from within the house. William was labelled by the magistrate 'a disgrace to humanity' and sentenced to six months in prison.

We do not know why or when Rose Callaghan became a prostitute, or if or when, or for what reason, she ever stopped. Rose's work and personal lives were clearly full of complexity, which kept her in a world of vice and danger. Like many other women who worked as prostitutes and returned repeatedly to communities saturated with violence, it was Rose's problematic relationships, desperate personal circumstances and lack of other viable options that held her in a life of suffering and offending. Unfortunately, those who advocated the suppression of vice sought only retribution against those responsible for causing public disorder and moral outrage, rather than offer any tangible change to the circumstances of women who lived with it.

Policing prostitutes: the Contagious Diseases Acts

The first Contagious Diseases Act was passed in 1864 and then expanded as the decade continued, with new amendments being passed in 1866 and 1869. This legislation made provision for the apprehension, detention and medical examination of any prostitutes suspected of having what we would refer to now as a sexually transmitted infection. In particular, the Acts sought to eradicate the spread of debilitating illnesses such as syphilis and gonorrhoea. The Acts came into being over concerns for the health of the armed forces. The Crimean War had reportedly seen more soldiers brought to camp hospitals suffering from the effects of venereal disease than injuries sustained on the battlefield. This was not only a military disaster but a considerable expense to the state also. The well-known liaisons between soldiers or sailors and prostitutes when the former were either on active service or on leave were identified as primarily responsible for the spread of these debilitating illnesses. As such, the Contagious Diseases Act placed strict regulations throughout select port and garrison towns in England and Ireland that restricted the operation and movements of prostitutes. The areas initially included were Portsmouth, Plymouth, Woolwich, Chatham, Sheerness, Aldershot, Colchester, Shorncliffe, and then Curragh, Cork and Queenstown in Ireland. By 1869, the Acts also included Canterbury, Dover, Gravesend, Maidstone, Devonport, Winchester and Windsor.

To stem the flow of contagious diseases thought to be spread by prostitutes, women were targeted. The Act stated:

> If any common prostitute is in any public place within the limits of any place to which this act applies, for the purpose of prostitution, and superintendent or inspector of Police or constabulary authorised to act in that place having good cause to believe that such common prostitute had a contagious disease may, by order in writing signed by him, direct a constable to take her into custody, and bring her, as soon as reasonably may be, before a Justice of the Peace, to be dealt with according to the law.

Once a woman was brought before a magistrate and it was ascertained by him that she was a 'common prostitute', the judge was able 'for the purpose of obtaining medical testimony as to her having a contagious disease, may, if he thinks fit, require her to be examined by a legally qualified medical practitioner.' If she were found to be infectious, such a woman would 'be taken to a certified hospital, there to remain until cured.' These hospitals became known as lock hospitals because they were closed wards where women could be detained against their will and forced to undergo compulsory internal examinations to determine the state of their sexual health. This procedure was so invasive that campaigners against the acts in the 1860s, 1870s and 1880s termed it 'instrumental rape'. If found to be suffering from the symptoms of a contagious disease the woman could be detained for up to six months and forced to undergo invasive medical procedures thought to be 'curative treatments' for their condition. Once a woman was judged to be 'clean', a certificate of good health would be issued to her and she would be released and free to resume her business.

The Contagious Diseases Acts were highly punitive towards women. Anything other than complete capitulation to the state on this matter was considered an offence. If a woman did not submit herself to this process, or was thought to be knowingly infected and not seeking help, she was liable to prosecution and imprisonment. If a woman continued to work as a prostitute in full knowledge that she had a contagious disease she was guilty of an offence. For a first offence she could be taken to prison for up to one month. For a second such offence she would be taken from the hospital and imprisoned for up to three months. If a woman left the lock hospital without consent she was likewise guilty of an offence and could be returned to the hospital indefinitely until deemed cured and then imprisoned for up to four months. While in the hospital, if a woman did not conform to the regulations of the ward, or if she refused examination or treatment, she could be imprisoned for a month. There were penalties too not just for the women who worked as prostitutes themselves, but for anyone running a house or room from which prostitutes operated who did not report infected women to the authorities. Brothel keepers could face a fine of up to £20 or up to six months in prison, with or without hard labour. It would also leave them liable for a separate prosecution for running a disorderly or 'bawdy' house. Later additions to the legislation also created restrictions on the movement of prostitutes within a 10-mile radius of the legislated areas.

The Contagious Diseases Acts left many prostitutes nowhere to hide. In affected districts any woman working the streets was liable to accusation and arrest, and brothels were not willing to risk expensive fines and unwanted attention from the police for the sake of any single prostitute. There are those who have suggested that the Contagious Diseases Acts were not solely concerned with irradiating venereal disease, but rather had a wider interest in controlling prostitution and punishing the women involved.

The Contagious Diseases Acts were cruel and discriminatory. They were also wholly unsuccessful. From a twenty-first century medical perspective it is clear that the treatments on offer to women suffering from sexually transmitted infections in the nineteenth century were ineffective. Thirty years prior to the discovery of penicillin – the most commonly used treatment for syphilis in the modern age – treatments for infected women were largely useless. From the frequent application of mercury, tannic acid or lotions containing sulphur to infected areas or open sores and daily hot baths, to internal and external chemical injections to the genitals, treatments given to women under the Contagious Diseases Acts were painful and invasive.

The failure of the Acts to eradicate sexual infections was occasioned by a mistake more fundamental than even the ineffective treatments. Those responsible for the legislation and running of the hospitals failed to realise that the spread of infection could only be controlled by methodical treatment of all of those affected. By targeting only women, men suffering from venereal diseases were left untreated and free to continue sexual activity and thus to infect other prostitutes, their wives or partners, and other men. Women given a certificate of clean health after treatment in a lock hospital were vulnerable to immediate reinfection if or when they resumed work.

The dismissal of the notion that men too might be apprehended and treated under the Contagious Diseases Acts is just one example of the persistent sexual double standard that faced all women – and prostitutes most especially. In the same way that only prostitutes were ever apprehended, publically shamed and prosecuted for their trade whilst their customers went free, only women were held responsible for the spread of sexually transmitted diseases. Such clear discrimination stemmed from the idea that female purity was essential to the delectate social balance. Women's chastity was required whilst male sexuality, virility and desire was perceived as a natural and inevitable part of masculinity. Any woman who engaged in pre-marital or extra-marital sex and, worse still, commercialised her sexuality was an utter corruption of all that was thought to be right and moral. It stood to reason that not only were such women responsible for the corruption of the streets, they could also be held solely accountable for the infection of the populace. In short, this deeply ingrained double standard fostered an understanding that men would naturally require the use of prostitutes and that such women had a responsibility to provide men with a clean and safe service, but that women who fulfilled this role should face moral and legal repercussions. As such, the rights and dignity of women working as prostitutes were not thought to merit concern.

The Acts, whilst only technically concerning certain areas, had a general impact on prostitution throughout England. The legislation allowed the police to target any woman with whom they had a pre-existing grievance on the grounds that they suspected her to have a contagious disease. The remit of the Acts over large swathes of the Home Counties and southern England effectively created a barrier around London that kept the mass of prostitutes working there from spreading out. Many felt that the geographical extent of the Acts was intended to curtail and contain the 'great social evil' to the capital. Prostitutes in London and, in fact, in most of the large metropolitan areas of England in this period came under increased scrutiny. They were harassed, arrested and driven from the streets.

One of the many problems caused by the Contagious Diseases Acts was in the identification of 'common prostitutes'. Given the numerous reasons and complex circumstances that drove women to work on the streets there was no single easily identifiable 'type' of prostitute. Those who dressed provocatively, who wore too much make-up, or touted indiscreetly for trade were easy to root out. However, most prostitutes were simply ordinary working women looking for a way to earn money. They were indistinguishable from the laundresses, factory workers, hawkers and charwomen who walked the roads, used the pubs and met on street corners. In essence, when police targeted 'common prostitutes' they could pursue any poor looking working women who were found to be in the wrong place at the wrong time or who were found to be behaving in a way that was perceived to be deviant.

One such case was reported from Liverpool in 1874, when a waitress left her place of work in Hope Street (a main thoroughfare in the town) after working the evening shift. She was accompanied home by a male acquaintance. A police constable saw the pair, a working-class woman and man together in the street at night, and took the situation for something more sinister than socialising. The constable attempted to arrest the woman as a 'disorderly prostitute' but she refused to go with him. A second constable was called to help with her apprehension and the protesting woman was much manhandled. Later, having taken the policemen's details, the woman was able to summon the first constable in front of a magistrate and prove her innocence. The police officer was admonished. Had it not been for her ability to prove she had been working that evening at a reputable establishment, she may well have been prosecuted, despite there being no evidence to suggest she was a prostitute or that she had venereal disease. Her only 'crime' was to be in the street, with a man, late in the evening. In both the areas where the Contagious Diseases Acts were technically in operation and in other areas like Liverpool, Leeds, London and Manchester, where the moral spirit of the acts had infiltrated policing practices, ordinary working-class women were vulnerable to wrongful identification as prostitutes and unfair treatment.

The Contagious Diseases Acts were active in England and Ireland for more than twenty years until their repeal in 1886. The repeal came only after a national outcry about the persecution of women and a lengthy campaign by several notable middle- and upper-class women who would go on to play prominent roles in the later campaign for female suffrage. The period during which the Acts operated saw women who worked as prostitutes come under the most intense scrutiny of the Victorian period. The Acts caused significant repercussions for the public perception of prostitutes, policing policy towards them and the experience of women who worked on the streets. The Contagious Diseases Acts did not stop the problem of sexually transmitted infections and neither did they make prostitution safer for women or hold their clients any more accountable. The legislation failed to supress prostitution by diminishing the clientele or addressing the social and economic reasons why so many women relied upon the trade. What the Acts did achieve was to further criminalise prostitutes and the sale of sex for money despite a lack of legal grounds. The Acts made the difficult life of many prostitutes even harder. Those who stuck to the streets despite heightened attention from the police faced prosecution more frequently. Others were driven from plain sight into the world of prostitution behind closed doors.

Brotheldom

By the middle of the nineteenth century, England had countless known and unknown prostitutes. The state pursued thousands of women through the courts each year for prostitution or related offences. Many were lone agents who worked the streets, alleyways and market places looking to earn a meagre living; others staffed the beer rooms and lodging houses that doubled as brothels. There were also those who inhabited boudoirs that serviced a more elite clientele: prostitution existed even for the wealthy and powerful. Some women were prostitutes who chose to work in the trade; other arrived at their hopeless situations by less voluntary means.

The majority of information we have about Victorian brothels comes from records of prosecution or social investigation. Overwhelmingly our evidence only allows us to focus on working-class female prostitution. It was more prominent in public awareness, more visible in an everyday setting than the clandestine wealthy equivalent, and less likely to relate to the personal interests of judges, politicians and newspaper editors. Nonetheless, in Victorian London, brothels existed in upmarket Knightsbridge as well as in lowly Whitechapel. The same claim can be made for almost anywhere in the country, even if we know less about the middle-class and elite sex industry.

Brothels were a key site of prostitution in England and could range in size and operation. They could be as basic as a back room of a residential dwelling where prostitutes lived and attended to customers away from prying eyes, to an entire property rented for providing prostitution. The precise number of such premises is unknown but likely to be vast. In Victorian cities and towns, no doubt more discreetly in rural areas too, there were formal brothels that could house anywhere from two to a dozen prostitutes at a time. More informal businesses, such as lodging houses or unlicensed beer halls, could also have resident prostitutes. They catered for out-of-town visitors, soldiers and sailors on leave looking for a place to spend the night, and for local working men who sought enjoyable ways to spend their weekly pay. A brothel could exist in almost any residential location. The nature of the brothel would reflect the intended clientele. Brothels were a fundamental part of prostitution throughout the period. They provided a way for women to carry on trading when the police routinely decided to clamp down on street prostitution, and offered prostitutes a guaranteed stream of customers at any time of year.

We most commonly think of prostitution as a trade run by men for men. We are familiar with violent street pimps who bullied and manipulated downtrodden women into serving the depraved appetites of Victorian gentlemen or drunken common labourers looking to spend a spare shilling. There is, of course, much evidence to suggest this occurred. The misery of sexual exploitation in the darkened streets and back rooms of England was not, however, without female influence. Women played a significant role in all levels of the Victorian sex trade. Women not only walked the streets and sold their bodies as 'common prostitutes' but also orchestrated and facilitated the exchange of sex for money. In most urban areas, women played a leading role in running the vast maze of brothels that housed the nation's prostitutes.

By 1860, there were upwards of 6,000 brothels known to authorities across England and Wales, concentrated in large towns and cities, particularly prominent in areas of Lancashire, Tyneside and London. In each of these 'houses of ill fame' a small number of women would receive bed, board and even clothing and jewellery in return for their services. Life in a brothel could offer prostitutes a certain amount of comradeship and support from other women in the same trade. It took them away from the disapproving eyes of the public and provided them with a basic level of safety from the violence of customers that lone street prostitutes did not have. Brothels offered women somewhere to ply their trade that included a very small semblance of home, complete with life's necessities, for a slice (or the vast majority) of their earnings. Yet far from providing a safe haven, brothels were also locations in which prostitutes met with violence, intimidation, coercion, extortion and exploitation. The prostitutes who staffed many brothels would have little say in whom or how many their customers were, and would quickly find that their earnings reverted directly to those that housed them. If prostitutes wanted to leave, proprietors made it difficult for them to do so. Prostitutes in brothels suffered acts of intimidation and violence and often left their positions with nothing – not the coins in their purses or sometimes even the clothes on their back. Once inside a brothel, a prostitute's prospect of leaving at her own free will was minimal. Successful 'madams' were shrewd businesswomen who were as capable of utilising fear and manipulation to keep their customers in line and employees docile as any male counterpart.

If a brothel became too notorious or caused too much disorder, the woman who ran it could be subject to prosecution, fines and imprisonment. She might also find herself prosecuted for making a dishonest or immoral living. Yet much like the legal grey area of prostitution, charging women to rent rooms in a house, which is what many brothel proprietors would claim they were doing, was not in itself an illegal act. Not that this would dissuade the police from making regular raids on and disbursements from the properties. It was not just because of prostitution that brothel keepers risked prosecution. Women who ran such establishments usually had multiple revenue streams through which they earned a living. A brothel made an ideal location from which to receive or trade in stolen goods or to sell alcohol illegally to customers. The crowded, dark and cramped streets in which multiple brothels might flourish put off the faint of heart and provided ideal cover for a range of illicit activities.

Old Cock Yard in Preston, home to Rose Callaghan, was just one small street behind the town's main station. However, the area was well known to the people and police of Preston alike as a centre of vice. In just this one street, from the 1850s to the 1890s, not only Rose but many dozens of women were charged with running brothels. Countless other women were likewise charged for the same in the neighbouring streets. On just one day in May 1857, for example, Alice Neeve, Esther Harrison, Elizabeth Harrison, Alice Booth and Elizabeth Howarth were all separately summoned for keeping brothels in Old Cock Yard.

Harriet Banks ran a brothel in the street for more than ten years. Over this time a large number of prostitutes, including Rose Callaghan, passed through her doors. In 1871, Harriet was brought to court for her part in a violent robbery. One of the prostitutes who worked in her house had taken a customer upstairs and as he undressed, Harriet robbed him of his waistcoat and money. In 1874, on a 'salutary raid on brothels', Harriet was issued a fine of ten shillings for the house that she kept. Harriet and others in the street who kept similar establishments, like Jane Williams and Elizabeth Slater, might be fined and bought to court for their businesses on almost a monthly basis, accumulating ten, twenty or thirty convictions. However, the short terms of imprisonment and small fines they faced were not enough to persuade them to close their houses or move from Preston. Available methods for catching and punishing those who ran brothels often proved frustrating for the police, too, who, other than bringing women to court to face these summary punishments, were largely powerless to clamp down on brothels, which were proving to be hotbeds of crime and disorder. Even if individual houses could be closed, others would only materialise within weeks.

In 1877, Harriet was charged with selling beer without a licence after the police entered her premises looking, in all probability, for a reason to apprehend her. They found several men there drinking beer from a jug. In 1881, Harriet worked with Rose Callaghan to rob items worth several pounds from Michael Smith. In 1883, she faced a charge of aiding and abetting an illicit trade in beer when she helped her neighbour who ran the Garth's Arms to supply beer to customers during prohibited hours. In 1890, Harriet and another brothel owner from Old Cock Yard were found guilty of having stolen money from a labourer as he entered their premises to 'enquire about lodgings'.

Old Cock Yard in Preston was not exceptional. Brothel districts existed all over urban England. Wherever there was enough passing footfall to make such endeavours lucrative, women would set up brothels. Although brothels close together competed for trade, the clustering of these establishments in 'no-go areas' provided a certain amount of convenience for the women who ran them.

Liverpool, renowned countrywide during the Victorian era as a centre of vice and sexual immorality, had a thriving brothel district. Such was the infamy of the area that the neighbourhood was simply referred to as 'Little Hell'. This area, which incorporated the streets behind and surrounding the town's central railway station, Lime Street, housed dozens of closely packed brothels along with pubs, lodging houses and dens where stolen property could be traded. A strict policing strategy in the earlier part of the nineteenth century had driven many of Liverpool's brothels and sites of vice into the slums surrounding the station. It was contended by many legal and political commentators that keeping the high concentration of brothels in this area was the only sure way to keep 'gay and disreputable characters' away from respectable people. It was felt that to scatter prostitutes and brothel owners out of their present haunts would be an 'aggravation of the evil' that would spread and infect the rest of the town. Thus, whilst the high concentration of 'undesirables' in these streets was a great source of anxiety to Liverpool's elite, to a large extent the multitude of problems in the area were left to stagnate.

In the 1880s alone, brothel keepers from Little Hell like Winifred Curran (see plate 23) and Margaret Gray were prosecuted for running their houses, supplying beer without a licence, theft and trafficking in stolen property, assault on the women that worked for them, assault against customers and, in Margaret Gray's case, even the murder of a customer in a robbery gone wrong. In a way, Little Hell was a place in which brothels presented women with the opportunities they were denied elsewhere in society. They could be business owners, independent operators and women with power. Here, women who ran brothels and controlled prostitutes were feared and respected members of their communities.

Procuring prostitutes

Brothel madams and the other women who worked with them didn't just run the rooms where prostitutes could be bought, they also fuelled the supply of women entering the trade. These women were known to the police and the press as 'procuresses'. They were those who selected girls and convinced or coerced them into selling sex for money. This could take place either in a procuress's own establishment or those of male and female associates. It was women who were those most often prosecuted in the courts for luring young girls from the safety of their homes and away from their acquaintances into prostitution, as well as for running the houses of immorality and disorder that imprisoned them.

A procuress could be a woman aged anywhere from her twenties to her sixties, but most commonly they were above the age of thirty. Some were former prostitutes themselves; those who through age or illness had been obliged to stop selling themselves and had begun to survive by selling others. The occupation of a procuress was to find the most lucrative women to use as prostitutes. In a saturated market this meant not just finding the most good-looking girls of the poorer classes but in particular the very young and the 'unspoiled'. Virginity carried the highest premium in the Victorian sex trade. Procuresses found women to fill a market in which, one journalist remarked, 'anything can be done for money, if you only know where to take it.' The unfortunate women procured for the trade were sometimes bought and sold for vast amounts of money, far more than most could ever hope to see in a lifetime, which went directly to agents and owners rather than the women themselves.

The most famous case of procurement in the period shocked English society, and even changed the law. Journalist W.T. Stead, editor of the *Pall Mall Gazette*, scandalised England when he printed his series of articles entitled 'The Maiden Tribute of Modern Babylon' in July 1885. The articles were an exposé of London's illicit trade in child virgins that horrified the respectable drawing rooms of England and made Stead an overnight sensation. There were those who praised him for his bravery and vision and those who sought to protect him from the criminal prosecution that followed. Others found him every bit as guilty of the exploitation of the young and vulnerable as those he sought to expose for buying and defiling virgins in London's brothels and backrooms. Stead's 'Maiden Tribute' was a call to the honourable men of the capital to protect their womenfolk from the advances and appetites of the less scrupulous amongst them.

Stead claimed to have worked undercover in order to discover the sexual exploitation of children in the capital, where a virgin of 'not thirteen years of age' could be bought, he contended, for just £5. He was aided in his very hands-on investigation by a procuress he employed. Rebecca Jarrett had the right connections to buy and sell children into 'white slavery'. Rebecca arranged to purchase a 13-year-old girl named Eliza Armstrong from her mother. Varied versions exist as to what Eliza's parents were told and how complicit they were in her fate. Whatever the agreed arrangement, for a few pounds Eliza was released into Rebecca Jarrett's care. Eliza was then medically examined to prove her 'innocence' and transported to a brothel, where she was drugged and left in a room for Stead to behold. The whole investigation was published in newspapers nationwide within a matter of days.

Because of the scandal arising from the publication, Stead has gone down in history, his name synonymous with investigative journalism. At the same time, it has been frequently overlooked that, at its heart, the 'Maiden Tribute' was a story about women. Men largely provided the demand and market for the exploitation of children and the vulnerable. However, it was women who constituted not only the exploited (like little Eliza Armstrong) but also, more often than not, those responsible for facilitating and profiting from that exploitation, too. Rebecca Jarrett had a story like countless other women who had surrendered their lives to prostitution. Rebecca had herself worked as a prostitute, and as she grew older she ran a brothel and facilitated the prostitution of other women.

Rebecca had later given up her life as a prostitute and brothel keeper and become a fervent member of the Salvation Army. It was through the network of social investigators and philanthropists connected with the organisation that she was introduced to William Stead. He convinced her to use her past experiences to help bring to light the plight of innocent women and girls throughout the country. Rebecca Jarrett was eventually sentenced to six months in prison for her part in the abduction of Eliza Armstrong. After her release, Rebecca travelled the country and further abroad offering repentant speeches about her troubled former life and her work with the Salvation Army. She devoted herself to the cause of rescuing other fallen women. Rebecca Jarrett and Eliza were not the only women to play a role in the 'Maiden Tribute'. The midwife who performed an invasive examination to confirm Eliza's virginity was a woman, so too was the owner of the brothel to which Eliza was transported and confined. The procurement of women and girls for the purposes of prostitution and the facilitation of the trade rested heavily on the shoulders of their fellow women.

For a time after the scandal of the 'Maiden Tribute' the trafficking of prostitutes became a dangerous pastime for women like Rebecca Jarrett. A change to the law in the form of the 1886 Criminal Law Amendment Act raised the age of consent from thirteen to sixteen and saw heavier penalties bestowed upon women caught procuring the very young. It was not enough to stop the trade altogether, or even slow it for long. Through Stead's exposé of the 1880s' London child sex trade, the figure of the procuress gained her most notoriety. She, like the prostitute, abortionist or murdering wife and mother, came to embody everything that was wrong and corrupt about the female criminal. Like almost every other female offender, the procuress was the inversion of what a good Victorian woman should be.

Of course, the problem of procurement was far bigger than just underage victims in London, and had a history stretching much further back than the 1880s. The female-driven trade in the young, the vulnerable and the valuable was a well-established business by the time Queen Victorian took the throne in 1837, and continued long after 'The Maiden Tribute of modern Babylon' was published. The procurement of prostitutes took place over decades throughout the country, and even saw the desperate and alone transported across Europe for a life of vice.

Madame Anna

One of the most detailed accounts of an international procuress comes from mid-nineteenth-century Liverpool. The city, long held to be one of England's worst locations for vice, was notorious for its high number of brothels and known prostitutes. Despite being a much smaller city than London, by the later decades of the nineteenth century, Liverpool was prosecuting almost as many prostitutes as the capital. Certainly, figures for prostitution in Liverpool far outstripped those of rural Lancashire and even nearby Manchester. It was in this flourishing hotspot of prostitution that a prolific trafficker known locally as 'Madame Anna' rose to prominence during the 1850s.

On 11 December 1857, a portly woman, around forty years of age and elegantly attired, was brought up to the stand. Read against her was a complicated charge:

> having kept and maintained a certain common, ill-governed, and disorderly house and having in the said house, for her lucre and gain, caused to come together certain persons, as well as men and women of evil name and fame, for the purpose of drinking and tippling and otherwise misbehaving themselves.

She uttered only one word, in a soft accent tinged with German and Yiddish that spoke not of contrition but of calm and confident victory: 'Guilty.'

The following Monday, Madame Anna, or Johanna, Anna or Hannah Rosenberg as she was also known, was again placed in the stand. She retrieved a handkerchief about her person and held it to her face. She appeared to be weeping. After a short consultation with her counsel, her composure was restored and a sentence was pronounced upon her in which the judge struggled to hide his displeasure:

Johanna Rosenberg, in this case there has been no trial, but you have pleaded guilty, so that the facts have been brought before me by statement of counsel and by affidavit; and I will say at the outset that many things have been mentioned which I am not at liberty to take into consideration. I am not at liberty, for one reason, because you have had no opportunity of answering them, and because you have not been put on your trial for those offences. I am therefore not at liberty to consider these things in the sentence I am about to pronounce. What you have confessed is that you have been guilty of keeping a disorderly house. Now, it appears that you, not being an Englishwoman, but a foreigner, have for five years or more resided in this town and kept a brothel. It appears that the inmates of that house for the most part were girls, young girls, English and foreign; and under your auspices, under your eye, and in your house, many immoralities have been practised, and much harm, no doubt, has been done. If, as it is alleged, young girls have been induced by you into a course of life attended by misery and ending in destruction, you have indeed much to answer for. There must be a heavy burden on your conscience if you rightly consider these things. A just sense of such conduct ought to fill you with apprehensions more serious than can attend the sentence of any earthly judge. However, I don't exactly know how these things are, and I can only deal – especially considering that you have surrendered yourself by your pleas, to justice – with what is certain against you; and considering how long you have carried on this brothel in this town, and how much mischief must have been done there, the sentence of the court is that you must be imprisoned and kept to hard labour for four calendar months, and in addition to that, pay to the Queen a fine of £25, and be further imprisoned until that fine is paid.

Hard labour was not to be taken lightly but Madame Anna had had a lucky escape. Had it not been for the entrance of a guilty plea things could have been much worse for her. Moral reformers were baying for her blood. A fine of £25 (the equivalent of more than £1,500 in today's currency) was heavy. For others of her class, or the women who worked for her, it would have been a virtual impossibility to raise the funds. But not for Madame Anna. She had expensive clothes and diamond jewellery. She could readily raise the sum. She ran a profitable business: the trade in human flesh.

Little is known about the early life of Johanna Rosenberg. This was partly down to practicalities; a Prussian Jewish immigrant in the mid-nineteenth century was unlikely to leave much of a paper trail. But it was also by design, for those engaged in illegal activities, anonymity was the key: the fewer details there were for the authorities to use in identification, the longer and easier a career in this business could be.

The first trace of Madame Anna in England is at the Leeds Borough Sessions in June 1850. In all likelihood she had been in the town and running a brothel for some time before coming to the attention of the authorities. Here, she was charged for keeping a disorderly house and ordered to pay £20 'sureties' so that she would be bound to appear before the court again when called upon for a proper trial. Pay she did, but shortly afterwards it appears that Madame Anna decided to cut her losses and leave the town behind her. She did not appear in court again in Leeds and by March of the next year was living at 18 Hotham Street, Liverpool, working as a 'Lodging House Keeper'. On the census night of that year, the only lodgers at Madame Anna's establishment were young women: Charlotte Bonsell, listed as aged twenty from Cheshire; Kate Watson, aged twenty from Dublin; and Martha Williams and Emma Seddon, both eighteen and Liverpool natives. Although reported as adults, it is far more likely that the women were younger than stated. The house Madame Anna ran was not just a lodging house; it was a brothel. However, it was not just any brothel; it was a brothel on one of the most notorious streets of Little Hell.

The notoriety of Madame Anna's work means that rare testimony from the women in her charge survives. One woman, known only as M.W., testified:

> I am eighteen years of age. In January 1854, I left Manchester and came to Liverpool, having been then going about six weeks, I became acquainted with Madame Anna, and went to reside in her house. In a few days she enquired

if I would like to go to Hamburg, and having found me several articles of gay clothing I consented to go on terms – should I not like to remain I would be brought back. In company with two other young females named Amelia and Jeannie, I proceeded with Madame Anna to Hamburg about the beginning of March. On our arrival we were taken to the house of ill-fame, kept by a Madame Rant. A man there came in and examined my teeth and feet along with the other two; on the following morning we were again examined by the surgeon. We were then conveyed to the police office and our names entered in a book. Amelia became very much excited through fright. She was conveyed to the hospital where she died six weeks afterwards, and I remained at Madame Rant's house a few days, when we wished to return, but we were told she had paid the sum of £48 [£2,800 in modern currency] for me and £36 [£2,100] for Jeannie and £10 [£585] for Amelia, in consequences of being sick, and that we should not be allowed to go until the sum was paid. I then became disobedient, and Madame Rant stripped me of all my clothes, and again sold me to a Mrs Winch, a person of the same calling, for the same amount. I then strove to escape, when I was taken to prison, and committed for ninety-six hours. I was again stripped of my clothes and jewels, after liberation, and provided of an old skirt, dress and mantle, when an English gentleman paid my passage back to Liverpool, after being there ten weeks. While in Hamburg the usage towards me was very bad, and a captain told me and two other English girls that if we could make our escape he would convey us back to England free of expense. I was too closely watched to do so; but Jeannie succeeded in making her escape, but under what circumstances I never could learn.

The trade went both ways. Unwitting girls from England (perhaps fresh from the workhouse or lured with the promise of a position in domestic service, or a neighbourhood girl with no one else to turn to) could be shipped to Hamburg and sold on, and girls from Hamburg could be purchased and brought to the brothel in Hotham Street. The girls that Madame Anna transported to and from the Continent were sold for less than the price of a single piece of jewellery that Madame Anna was often reported as wearing. Madame Anna was finely adorned. She often wore trademark pieces such as a gold bracelet worth £35 (over £2,000 now) and a 'pin in the form of a snake set with diamonds' worth an incredible £55 (over £3,000).

In 1854, the *Yorkshire Gazette* reported, under the title, 'IMPORTATION OF GIRLS FROM GERMANY':

At Liverpool on Friday the attention of two magistrates was for some time engaged in hearing a charge preferred against Madame Anna Rosenberg, a notorious procuress, of detaining the clothes of a young girl named Anna Margarita Hesser, who was seduced from Hamburg about six months ago, but has now made her escape from the house of Madame Anna on Sunday night last. When she left Hamburg she was accompanied by a 'gentleman' who said he would procure her a better situation than the one she occupied (manager of a hotel) as well as with another girl who was also misled as to the intentions of the seducer ... the case was dismissed.

Young female virgins fetched a premium price in the right circles, and the evidence suggests that Madame Anna moved in all of them. Far from the street trade that frequented most brothels, Madame Anna had a select clientele. A witness testified:

When Madame gets a new girl she walks them through the town, especially through the exchange, and drops her card at the feet of her usual customers, who understand the sign.

Madame Anna serviced a more refined clientele than those of her neighbouring establishments and reaped all the benefits of doing so. It was not that the authorities were unaware of her crimes, or those of the many women throughout the country just like her, it was more likely that they were unwilling to curtail them. In 1853, Madame Anna found herself in court testifying as a witness in a case of debt to a jeweller, her business an open secret, her powerful connections protecting her. The newspaper reported:

Witnesses knew 'Madame Anna' ... She was a customer of his and he had lent her jewellery. He had been at her house in Hotham Street, and he thought the street was a respectable one. (Laughter.) He saw respectable people in it. Madame Anna was a respectable woman so far as he knew. (Renewed laughter.) He did not know that the jewellery lent to persons such as Madame Anna was for the purposes of prostitution.

Over the years, tales of violence, coercion and cruelty began to emerge from Madame Anna's establishment, which a constable later testified as 'the worst in the neighbourhood'. She faced few if any reprisals. In fact, reports show us that Madame Anna's business was thriving. Her notorious trade and reign over Hotham Street lasted for at least six years before the town was forced to act. A prosecution was eventually brought against her by the Society for the Suppression of the Vicious Practices. Evidence and affidavits were carefully collected and a warrant for her arrest was issued in the autumn of 1857. Madame Anna was apprehended fresh off the boat from Hamburg, with three new girls from Belgium in tow whom she had 'deluded' into following her.

When Madame Anna was brought to hear the charges against her, she would have faced a hostile courtroom with a variety of observers waiting to see her sentenced. There were the reformers who hoped to see the streets swept of the 'evil' of prostitution, eager police officers waiting to see long-awaited justice done, but friends too and perhaps even nervous clients. By pleading guilty to the first charges, and very possibly by having friends in the right places, Madame Anna avoided a damaging trial, further charges and a longer stay in prison.

Madame Anna was released from prison in the spring of 1858 and, as she had done before, she wasted no time in quitting the city. An imprisonment was a sure sign that the climate of the town had changed and that her business could no longer prosper unhindered. Perhaps she stayed in England and plied her trade in the similar house she was rumoured to keep in London. A woman of the same name and age died in Paddington in 1886; it may have been her. Alternatively, perhaps Madame Anna, or Johanna Rosenberg, changed her name and continued to ply her trade in a new city, with new customers and new impunity. Sensing the shape of things to come Madame Anna may have even fled back to her native Prussia and continuted to fuel the European trade in women from the Continent.

Although Madame Anna disappeared, taking her connections with her, there were many others ready to step into her shoes. None of them made quite the newspaper headlines that Madame Anna had, but scores of women just as ruthless and as capable as she existed throughout England; they procured women to fill their brothels and ruled prostitutes and clients alike with an iron fist. The trade in young women within England and between England and the Continent was well established. Madame Anna was by no means the first, and was certainly not the last. The year before her downfall, a woman identified only as a 'Belgian Jewess' was tried amid much sensation for running a trade in girls between London and Hamburg.

The actions of women like Johanna Rosenberg and Rebecca Jarrett continued to the close of the nineteenth century. The national outcry caused by Stead's 'Maiden Tribute' saw multiple cases tried in 1886 alone. For example, in 1886, Frenchwoman Eugene Rouiller was tried in a high profile case at the Old Bailey for attempting to procure a girl under the age of twenty-one for 'immoral purposes', taking her to Paris. In the same year, at the same court, a Louisa Hart was sentenced to five years' penal servitude 'for procuring Rosie Shires, aged thirteen, for prostitution'. Likewise, Julia Green, originally from Hamburg, was brought to court for running similar brothels to those of Madame Anna at Tottenham Court Road. Not only had Julia been running the brothel for ten years, full of women from England and Europe, but many of the local police officers at her trial had enjoyed 'drinks' at her establishment. On top of running a brothel at 45 Burton Crescent, Julia was also accused of running a disorderly house at numbers 27 and 28 of the same street.

On the surface, Victorian society was most preoccupied with protecting virtue and guarding women against the evils of vice and impropriety. From an early age, women were taught to beware of the worldly male seducer who would come with promises and presents to trick them out of their virtue and leave them ruined. For this reason, the work of procuring unwitting women to fill the brothels and streets of England as prostitutes was uniquely, and perhaps surprisingly, women's work. The role of a procuress demanded the art of obtaining false confidence; it was work of delicate deception. The procuress lured young and vulnerable girls away from friends and family. She was allowed to select and spirit away otherwise unwanted girls at will from orphanages and workhouses. To carry out these acts repeatedly without raising suspicion was no mean feat. A procuress was successfully able to convince those who had, in most cases, never left their home town to leave the country. She would elicit a feeling of safety and trust in her victims. Women were those ideally placed to carry out such work. The mature women who came with offers of a home, fine clothes, adventure and the care of new friends, were able to lure others away from safety without so much as a raised eyebrow until, in most cases, it was far too late.

If any Victorian offender can be said to have been the proverbial wolf in sheep's clothing, it was the procuress.

A woman's world?

Prostitutes are some of the most well known and easily recognisable wayward women of the Victorian period. From the bawdy street walker of Dickensian fiction to the child 'slaves' who were the subject of the newspaper exposé of the century, prostitution saturated the national consciousness. Female prostitutes themselves were the subject of scorn and scandal and, only very occasionally, pity. Most prostitutes were not the characters of stage and screen; they were women contending with their own personal tragedies, crises and addictions.

Sadly, prostitution rarely saw an end to women's troubles, instead confronting them with new ones – legal, personal, and even political. The battle waged against 'immorality' and prostitution throughout the Victorian period served only to punish women who worked as prostitutes, making their hard lives still more difficult, and doing nothing to tackle the root causes that drove women into the trade.

That woman's primary role in the Victorian sex trade was as a commodity to be bought and sold in an illicit marketplace is hard to dispute. However, working on the 'front line' as prostitutes was not the only role that women played. Women's agency extended past the transaction between prostitute and client as they took opportunities to run locations in which sex and money were exchanged, and even took responsibility for procuring new women to work in the trade.

Women who worked as prostitutes undoubtedly experienced manipulation, exploitation and victimisation, which drove them to and kept them in the trade against their wills. Their stories have remained prominent, in fact and fiction, to illicit our sympathies still in the twenty-first century. Yet, to appreciate fully how prostitution operated in Victorian England we must remember that for the women living the tragic reality of Dickens's Nancy, there were others playing the roles of Bill Sykes and Fagin also.

Conclusion

We have only begun to scratch the surface of the long list of activities that brought Victorian female offenders into contact with the police and courts. Yet even our introduction shows that there was far more complexity to the world of female offending than Victorian fiction and modern-day stereotypes would have us believe. Famous stories, real or fictional, show us only a fraction of what was taking place in the cities, towns and villages of England.

Some familiar faces have their place within the history of women and crime. Tragic street-working prostitutes were more than just the stuff of novels, nimble young women did take to the streets to pick pockets and snatch bags, and women who turned to shoplifting when necessity demanded came from all classes. They all have something to teach us about the lives and times of offenders in this era. As to whether these women should dominate the history of female offending, the answer is, quite simply, no.

We have seen that whatever corner of Victorian crime and deviance we look to women were there perpetrating all manner of offences against person, property and public order. Women could be abusive wives and desperate mothers, fierce combatants and angered lovers who turned to extreme violence. They were con artists, muggers, land sharks, child strippers and coiners. Repeat offenders could easily be made of women battling alcoholism, homelessness and desperation.

Women's role in the sex trade went much further than solely the prostitutes that made a difficult living on England's streets. In the majority of cases, female offenders were not only those that had broken England's criminal laws. Female deviance also posed a serious threat to the cultural ideals and moral sensibilities of the Victorian age. Many of the crimes we have seen that women could turn their hands to involved the inversion of social and gender norms. When male offenders transgressed the law, they became bad characters and convicts but, importantly, they remained in line with social understandings of male behaviour and masculinity. When a woman offended, she could be perceived as not only criminal but also as a Victorian 'anti-woman'. Female acts involving deception, violence and unchecked sexuality scandalised Victorian society because they challenged ideas that women were inherently weak, dull-witted, passive and pure. If the tales of wayward women in this book have shown us anything, it is that when it came to being offenders, more often than not, women could be ruthless, daring, brutal, unashamed and highly active. Female offenders were not hapless molls who acted as little more than the puppets of their male acquaintances. Women were more than capable of pursuing their own agenda when it came to crime and deviance.

So where does this leave us? The tales of the theft, violence and disorder of Victorian women are remarkable, but at the same time somehow chillingly ordinary. Much of the time, stories of female offenders are sad and thought provoking rather than glamourous or dramatic. The world we live in is a very different one to that inhabited by Victorian England's wayward women. Access to healthcare, childcare, education, better opportunities for employment and a living wage have all improved the lives of women and reduced the circumstances that saw women gravitate towards crime. More importantly, slow but steady change in how women are treated and perceived has altered the way in which women interact with society and the law. In turn, this changed the rate and nature of female offending. However, far away as the world of Victorian wayward women may seem, there are also startling continuities to be found amongst their tales of loss, hardship and desperation. If we could take one lesson from these women, it would be that in any time all that is required for the most shocking or mundane of crimes to thrive is a toxic mix of poverty, neglect and social exclusion.

On that note, it seems only right that the final word on this matter should not be my own, but that of someone with first-hand experience of Victorian England's offenders – author of *In Darkest England*, William Booth:

> How strange it is that so much interest should be excited by a narrative of human squalor and human heroism in a distant continent, whilst greater squalor and heroism not less magnificent may be observed at our very doors.

For the Intrigued Reader

The stories captured in the pages of this book are but a small proportion of all there is to know about the women (and men) offending all over Victorian England and beyond. During my years of researching the history of crime, I have drawn inspiration from the work of numerous historians, and had at my fingertips some fantastic resources. The following suggestions for reading, primary material and inspiration are available for any reader, researcher or budding historian who wants to know more.

Primary material

Old Bailey Proceedings (www.oldbaileyonline.org)
For more than ten years, Old Bailey Online has constituted one of the most important resources for those interested in crime and criminal justice in England from the seventeenth to the twentieth century. These free-to-access and fully searchable trial proceedings allow an unparalleled glimpse into the courtroom, and surviving ordinary's accounts can even take us all the way to the gallows. The Old Bailey Online provides the opportunity to learn about the crime and punishment of Victorian London. Transcriptions of cases offer the chance to get a feel for court life and how, in their own words, offenders, prosecutors and witnesses told the story of offending.

British Newspaper Archive (www.britishnewspaperarchive.co.uk)
The largest digitised collection of historic newspapers available in Britain, this database provides more than 200 years' worth of newspapers from across Britain and Ireland. Most of those published during the Victorian period contain weekly (if not daily) accounts of crime and punishment, which can be searched for the name of an individual offender or incidents of a particular kind of offence.

Tasmanian Archives (www.linc.tas.gov.au)
The free-to-access online collections provided by the Tasmanian Archives provide a first-hand history of convicts in Australia. Conduct records and physical descriptions of convicts allow us to follow those transported across the seas for punishment, whilst birth, marriage and death records provide the opportunity to see what lives convicts made for themselves after their sentences were over.

Research

The Digital Panopticon (www.digitalpanopticon.org)
The research in this book has been greatly enhanced by the work and resources provided by The Digital Panopticon project. The website (still under development at time of writing but due for completion at the end of 2017) provides details of the lives and experiences of thousands of women, men and children sentenced at London's Central Criminal Court to either transportation to Australia or imprisonment in England. As well as new records and information relating to the lives and crimes of convicts The Digital Panopticon provides resource pages for those interested in pursuing convict research of their own.

WaywardWomen (www.waywardwomen.wordpress.com)
My own blog on the history of female offenders provided the inspiration and opportunity for this book. Topics include all things gender and crime related, including the diverse activities of England's female offenders and their punishments and tales of the complex personal lives that set women on a pathway to crime. WaywardWomen offers a miscellany of research on women, crime and society in the nineteenth and twentieth centuries.

Criminal Historian (www.criminalhistorian.com)
This blog presents some fascinating case studies of English crime spanning the eighteenth and nineteenth centuries. Nell Darby draws on her extensive knowledge of crime reporting, the English magistracy and social history to report on the weird and wonderful world of crime and deviancy.

Reading

Non-fiction from the nineteenth century

Acton, W., *Prostitution Considered in its Moral, Social and Sanitary Aspects*, John Churchill, London, 1857.

Booth, C., *Labour and Life of the People*, Williams & Norgate, London, 1891.

Booth, W., *In Darkest England and the Way Out*, Salvation Army, London, 1890.

Engels, F., *The Condition of the Working Class in England in 1844*, S. Sonnenschein, London, 1892.

Maybrick, F., *Mrs Maybrick's Own Story: My Fifteen Lost Years*, Funk & Wagnalls Company, London, 1905.

Mayhew, H., 'London Labour and the London Poor', vol. IV, London, 1861.

Fiction

Dickens, C., *Oliver Twist* or *The Parish Boy's Progress*, Richard Bentley, London, 1839.

Hardy, T., *Tess of the D'urbervilles*, James R. Osgood, McIlvaine & Co, London, 1891.

Modern histories of women and of crime

Archer, J., *The Monster Evil: Policing and Violence in Victorian Liverpool*, University of Liverpool Press, 2011.

Cox, P., *Gender, Justice and Welfare: Bad Girls in Britain, 1900–1950*, Palgrave Macmillan, Basingstoke, 2003.

Davies, A., *The Gangs of Manchester*, Milo, Preston, 2008.

D'Cruze, S., *Crimes of Outrage: Sex, Violence and Victorian Working Women*, University College London Press, 1998.

Finnegan, F., *Poverty and Prostitution: A Study of Victorian Prostitutes in York*, Cambridge University Press, 1979.

Gray, D., *London's Shadows: The Dark Side of the Victorian City*, Continuum, London, 2010.

Hartman, M., *Victorian Murderesses: A True History of Thirteen Respectable French and English Women Accused of Unspeakable Crimes*, Robson Books, London, 1985.

Hughes, R., *The Fatal Shore: A History of the Transportation of Convicts to Australia 1787–1868*, Collins Harvill, London, 1987.

Knelman, J., *Twisting in the Wind: The Murderess and the English Press*, University of Toronto Press, 1998.

McConville, S., *English Local Prisons, 1860–1900: Next Only to Death*, Routledge, London, 1995.

Meier, W., *Property Crime in London 1850–Present*, Palgrave Macmillan, Basingstoke, 2011.

Oxley, D., *Convict Maids: The Forced Migration of Women to Australia*, Cambridge University Press, 1996.

Priestley, P., *Victorian Prison Lives: English Prison Biography, 1830–1914*, Pimlico, London, 1999.

Samuel, R., *East End Underworld: Chapters in the Life of Arthur Harding*, Routledge & Keegan Paul, London, 1981.

Thomas, D., *The Victorian Underworld*, John Murray, London, 1998.

Walkowitz, J., *City of Dreadful Delight: Narratives of Sexual Danger in Late-Victorian London*, University of Chicago Press, 1992.

Walkowitz, J., *Prostitution and Victorian Society: Women, Class, and the State*, Cambridge University Press, 1980.

Watson, K., *Poisoned Lives: English Poisoners and their Victims*, Hambledon & London, London, 2004.

Zedner, L., *Women, Crime and Custody in Victorian England*, Oxford University Press, 1992.

Index